THE ISLANDMAN

TOMÁS Ó CROHAN WITH HIS BOOK

THE ISLANDMAN

TOMÁS Ó CROHAN

TRANSLATED FROM THE IRISH

BY

ROBIN FLOWER

OXFORD
AT THE CLARENDON PRESS

Oxford University Press, Ely House, London W. 1

GLASGOW NEW YORK TORONTO MELBOURNE WELLINGTON
CAPE TOWN IBADAN NAIROBI DAR ES SALAAM LUSAKA ADDIS ABABA
DELHI BOMBAY CALCUTTA MADRAS KARACHI LAHORE DACCA
KUALA LUMPUR SINGAPORE HONG KONG TOKYO

ISBN 0 19 815202 7

First edition by The Talbot Press, Dublin
and by Chatto & Windus 1937
Published in Penguin Books, 1943
Printed at the University Press, Oxford, 1951
Reprinted 1958, 1963, 1965, 1967, 1971 (twice)
1972, 1974

Printed in Great Britain
at the University Press, Oxford
by Vivian Ridler
Printer to the University

FOREWORD

THE book here translated was first published in 1929, and had an immediate success among readers of Irish. It was the first attempt by a peasant of the old school, practically uneducated in the modern sense, though highly trained in the tradition of an ancient folk culture, to set out the way of his life upon his remote island from childhood to old age. This attempt had an interest of its own, but the fascination of the result was greatly enhanced by the unique individuality of the writer, who, though sharing to the full in the character and interests of the community in which he grew up, was peculiarly adapted by the whole bent of his mind to act as an observer as well as a vigorous participant in all the events of his isolated world. That little world—the island group of the Blaskets lying off the extreme point of the peninsula of Corcaguiney in West Kerry—he nowhere attempts to describe. And it may be of use to the reader unacquainted with that part of Ireland to have before him some brief account of the natural environment of the life depicted in this book. The peninsula of Corcaguiney runs out west into the Atlantic between the two bays of Dingle and Tralee. It is a wild world of intertangled mountains, culminating in the great mass of Brandon, beyond Dingle. West of Mount Brandon again two hills, the pointed shape of Croaghmartin and the long body of Mount Eagle, divide the two parishes of Ventry and Dunquin, and beyond Dunquin, to the north, lies the parish of Ballyferriter. In the old days the approach to Dunquin, to which parish the Blaskets belong, was by the hill pass that climbs between these two summits. But in the days of the great famine a relief road was constructed round the promontory of Slea Head under Mount Eagle, and the heavier traffic now takes that way. Going by the old road, you see below you, as you top the pass, the parish of Dunquin, and, out in the sea beyond, the six main islands of the group. Nearest to the land lies Beginish —a small flat island of good grass. A mile to the west is the Great Blasket—a high, narrow island, three miles by one, with a little cluster of houses on its eastern front towards the mainland, perched on the cliff above the tiny harbour and the long beach of sand called An Tráigh Bhán, the White Strand. Beyond the White Strand to the north there is a cliff-ringed beach of shingle known as the Gravel Strand, on which boats may be pulled up. Here the island sheep are driven for shearing, and on the rocks, out from the beach, weed is gathered for manure. The adventure of the women in Chapter 2 happened here, and here Tomás had his encounter with the seal (Chapter 9). The island rises westward in a series of hills on which the cattle and sheep find scant pasturage and rabbits burrow in the lofty cliffs. The best turf in the island is on its summit, on the hill called Sliabh an Dúna, beyond the prehistoric cliff fort which gives its name to the height, and a rough road leads some way back along the island in that direction. Above the road is an old martello tower, dating from the French wars, which stood unimpaired until a few years ago, when a thunderbolt shattered it. At the end of the island the hill falls away into a grassy expanse, slanting to the south, where was an ancient settlement, of which only fragments of beehive dwellings now remain. Beyond this again the land narrows, and you climb over jagged rocks to Ceann Dubh, Black Head, the extreme western point of the island. A narrow strait separates Ceann Dubh from Inish na Bro, Quern Island, and a little farther off lies Inishvickillaun, where is an ancient church and a little modern house, now only intermittently inhabited. The caves of Ceann Dubh and Inishvickillaun are haunted by seals, and Inish na Bro and Inishvickillaun teem with rabbits. Farther out to the west is the Teeraught, the Western Island, a high pinnacle of rock carrying a lighthouse, the last light that Irish emigrants see on their voyage to America. North of the main island is Inish Tooshkert, the Northern Island, a fastness of cliffs, in which is a well-preserved ancient oratory.

These islands and the seas about them are the theatre of the events described in this book. They are inhabited by a small population of fishermen of comparatively recent mainland origin, who support themselves precariously by fishing and on the produce of their fields and flocks. Their church is in Dunquin, their market-town is Dingle, and few of the older inhabitants have ever ventured farther east than Tralee. They are all Irish speakers, and, though English is taught in the little school, it has made no way in the common intercourse of the island. The older inhabitants have a rich store of folk-tale and folk-song, and in the period described in this book the little community was a typical example of an Irish village of the old fashion, practically untouched by modern influences. The great value of this book is that it is a description of this vanishing mode of life by one who has known no other, and tells his tale with perfect frankness, serving no theory and aiming at no literary effect, but solely concerned to preserve some image of the world that he has known, or, in his own words, 'to set down the character of the people about me so that some record of us might live after us, for the like of us will never be again'.

For the purposes of such a record Tomás was admirably fitted by a long and unconscious preparation. It will be clear to every reader that from his earliest days he was keenly observant, watching and judging the people about him, eagerly alive to their tricks of character, and appreciating to the full the humours and tragedies of their life. He has always been a handy man, meeting with ready

expedients every call on sea or land and scornfully critical
of the left-handed blunderings of the less expert among his
fellows. Life on such an island, where there are no shops
and no craftsmen at call, develops an all-round compe-
tence in the individual to which our specialized civiliza-
tions afford no parallel. The experience of these islanders
is necessarily narrow in its range, but within that range it
is absolute and complete. At sea and on the hill, in the
house, in the field, or on the strand, they must at all times
be prepared for every event. There is always a narrow
margin between them and famine or violent death, and
their faculties are the keener for that. All this necessary
equipment of an islandman is raised to a higher power in
Tomás by a natural critical faculty. He has always reflected
on his experience and watched his fellows with a certain
aloofness. A not unfriendly irony distinguishes his conversation and gives a sharp flavour to many of the pictures in
his book. He has an inborn sense of decency and restraint,
and in the wild scenes of carousal, which are the inevitable
relief demanded by the monotonous and restricted life of a
community imprisoned by the sea, he will be seen observ-
ing a quiet moderation and watching lest his more reckless
companions come to any harm.

This critical alertness is very noticeable in his use of his
native language. Those who, like myself, have had the
privilege of his friendship and instruction have often
wondered at the neatness and precision of his explanations
of the meaning of words and phrases, his ready produc-
tion of synonyms and parallels out of a vast vocabulary,
the finish and certainty of his phrasing in ordinary conversation.

There has always been a strong literary tradition among
the Munster peasantry. They have preserved orally a considerable corpus both of folk-song and of the more elabo-
rate poetry of the eighteenth century. And their folk-tales

are related by the best exponents in a fascinating idiom which has a natural quality of literature. All this tradition Tomás inherits from the poets and taletellers with whom he consorted eagerly in his young days. The island poet may have made him suffer, but he taught him much. And his own inborn genius for speech has refined his acquirements into an individual style. He has told me that, in writing this book, he aimed at a simple style, intelligible to every reader of Irish, using none of the 'cruadh-Ghaoluinn', the 'cramp-Irish' of the pure literary tradition. This aim he has achieved. For the narrative runs easily in the ordinary language of the island, with only an occasional literary allusion of a straightforward kind. But the style is none the less unmistakably his own, and to those who have known the man his whole figure and character is implicit in the manner of his writing.

If I may speak for myself, the reading of this book brought vividly to my mind my earliest experience of the author, when he was in his strength, over twenty years ago. He was in those days a small, lively man, with a sharp, intelligent face, weathered and wrinkled by the sun and rain and the flying salt of the sea, out of which two bright, observant eyes looked critically upon the world. He was then hard at work, fishing and helping to build houses for the Congested Districts Board, but he spared the time to help me with my studies. Lying under the lee of a turf-rick, or sitting in his own house or the King's kitchen, he would pour out tales and poetry and proverbs, quickening the whole with lively comments and precise explanations of difficult words and interspersing memories of his own life and of the island past. If this experience had been forgettable, this book, which gives so vivid a picture of the man, would have brought it back to me. And I can only hope that my attempt at translation does not fail too hopelessly to convey this double image.

For the method adopted in this translation a word of excuse may be offered. Irish and English are so widely separated in their mode of expression that nothing like a literal rendering from the one language to the other is possible. It is true that there has come into being a literary dialect, sometimes used for translation from Irish or for the purpose of giving the effect of Irish speech, which in books or on the stage has met with considerable applause. And in skilful hands this mixture of Irish and English idioms has often an effect of great charm. It does not to my ear, however, convey the character of the language as naturally spoken by those to whom it is their only speech. There is always something slightly artificial about it, and often a suggestion of the pseudo-poetic. This literary dialect could not be used to render the forthright, colloquial simplicity of the original of this book. For the same reason the more sophisticated forms of literary English are also excluded. It seemed best therefore to adopt a plain, straightforward style, aiming at the language of ordinary men who narrate the common experiences of their life frankly and without any cultivated mannerism. The constant charm of Irish idiom, which is so delightful in the original, must necessarily be lost. But rouge is no substitute for a natural complexion.

A few words may be added on the genesis of the original book. It would probably never have occurred to Tomás to write his life, had it not been for Mr. Brian O'Kelly of Killarney, who encouraged him to set about the work, and read over part of Maxim Gorki's autobiography to him to show the interest of that kind of writing. The book was written in a series of letters to Mr. O'Kelly. This accounted for the bulk of the matter. These letters Mr. O'Kelly handed over to Mr. Sugrue, who, under the name of 'An Seabhac', has published a series of delightful tales in the language of West Kerry. Tomás then wrote the remaining part of the book, and it was published under Mr. Sugrue's editorship, and in the Irish form met with immediate success. My own thanks are due to Mr. Sugrue, who has been kind enough to read over this translation. The photographs by Mr. Thomas H. Mason of Dublin are reproduced by his kind permission.

ROBIN FLOWER

CONTENTS

xiv   *Contents*

LIST OF PLATES

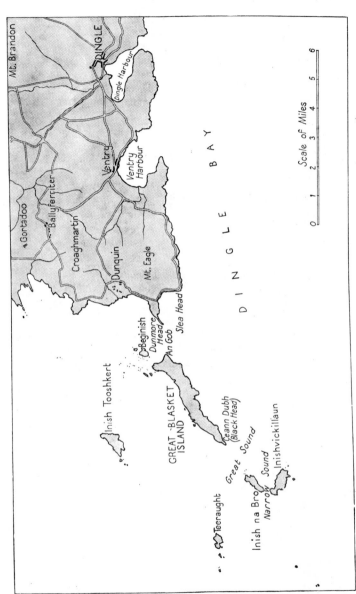

THE BLASKET ISLANDS

1. *My Childhood*

I WAS born on St. Thomas's day in the year 1856. I can
recall being at my mother's breast, for I was four years old
before I was weaned. I am 'the scrapings of the pot', the
last of the litter. That's why I was left so long at the breasts.
I was a spoilt child, too.

Four sisters I had, and every one of them putting her
own titbit into my mouth. They treated me like a young
bird in the nest. Maura Donel, Kate Donel, Eileen Donel,
and Nora Donel—those were their names. My brother was
Pats Donel, and I am Tomás Donel. Maura is living still in
this island,[1] two of them are still alive in America, and Pats
isn't dead yet. Kate died after drawing the old-age pension
for three months. That was the whole bunch of us. They
were all well grown when I was a baby, so that it was little
wonder that I was spoilt among them all. Nobody expected
me at all when I came their way.

My father was a middle-sized man, stout and strong.
My mother was a flourishing woman, as tall as a peeler,
strong, vigorous, and lively, with bright, shining hair. But
when I was at the breast there was little strength in her
milk, and besides that I was 'an old cow's calf', not easy to
rear. For all that, the rascal death carried off many a fine
young ruffian and left me to the last. I suppose he didn't
think it worth his while to shift me. I was growing stronger
all the time and going my own way wherever I wanted,
only that they kept an eye on me to see that I didn't go

[1] Died December 1923.

by the sea. I wore a petticoat of undressed wool, and a knitted cap. And the food I got was hens' eggs, lumps of butter, and bits of fish, limpets, and winkles—a bit of everything going from sea or land.

We lived in a cramped little house, roofed with rushes from the hill. Often the hens would nest in the thatch and lay a dozen eggs there. We had a post bed in the corner, and two beds at the bottom of the house. There used to be two cows in the house, the hens and their eggs, an ass, and the rest of us. Our house was reversed: that is, its door faced north—all the others were turned to the south.

There was another house opposite with its door towards us, and the two families chattered together every day. The woman from that house was in and out of our house all day long. She always had something as a result of her visits. She was a little, undersized, untidy-haired babbler with a sallow face, not much to look at—a gossip, always hither and thither. She was always saying to my mother that all Ireland couldn't rear an old cow's calf, and I don't think any cow, old or young, ever had a more wretched-looking calf than herself. But all the same, she had a good heart.

I was soon sprouting finely, and the grey petticoat was getting too short for me. I was coming to know things then. I took the measure of the old girl opposite pretty soon, and gave her tit for tat. The two families used to be in our house every Sunday when my father said the Rosary. The woman from the house across the way used to say to my mother every Sunday: 'You'll leave the grey petticoat on him till you're looking for a wife for him. Isn't he growing at a rate, God bless him!', so she would say, with a great lump of a bream safe in her stomach.

My father's kin were from Dunquin. He married into the Island. My mother's people were from Ventry. They were both willing to take one another. They hadn't the way that some couples have that makes you want to take a stick to them to make them marry! They settled down in a little cabin to live on the produce of the sea, and they had a bit of land, too; and both of them were well gifted to make the best profit out of sea and land. There were no asses in the Island in those days, only a creel on the back of every man—and of every woman, too—that is to say, every woman that wasn't a pet or a sly knave who would rather starve than work.

My father was a marvellous fisherman and a great man for work. He was a stonemason and boat's captain, and handy at every trade. He often did a hand's turn for other folk, for in those days most of them were little better than a drove of asses in a field. It was a great year for fish, that year when I wore the grey petticoat, and was still throwing an odd glance now and again at my mother's breast, for I had a fancy that I ought to be dragging at the teats still. I suppose that they weren't more than two years behind me that time.

One morning my father was going out fishing. They had a fine rick of turf on the hill, well on in the year, and they had been told that all the turf had been stolen the day before. He told my mother to do her best to bring some of the turf home, for the day was fine. She threw the creel on her back, and had brought back six creels of turf before the pet woke out of his slumbers. She had to leave the turf alone then and lend an ear to him now he was awake. She dressed me in the grey petticoat and gave me a bite to eat, and, though I ought to have been contented, I wasn't. My mother set the creel straight to make for the hill again, but I had my eye on her and she had to let me go with her. I could only make a shift at climbing the hill, crawling on all fours sometimes, and I soon grew tired, so that she was forced to throw me into the creel and carry me up the hill. She cursed me once or twice, and I don't blame her.

When she had filled up the creel with the turf, she signed

to me to be making my way down hill, but I made more fuss about going back than I had about coming. I remember well that she put the toe of her foot under me and lifted me clear off the ground to help me well away, and said: 'Bad cess to you, you've made a fine muddle of the day on me.' She had to carry me home in front of her with the creel at her back as full as it had ever been before. She dropped me on the floor, and told Maura to shove me under a creel and leave me there to live or die. For all the tricks I played, she brought down a score of creels that day, and by Sunday she had the whole great rick of turf safely housed. My father got five thousand fish that week. My mother would be telling these tales to the old hag over the way.

A hard year came about the time when I was still very young. A ship was wrecked that year on the north side of the Island. The ship was ground to smithereens, and her cargo—some kind of palm-oil it was—went afloat in lumps all over the sea. It was valuable stuff, and very little of it would bring a poor man a half sack of white meal—yellow meal hadn't come in at that time. There were coastguards in Dunquin in those days, and there was need of them, for ships were always being driven in on the coast, as there was no other contrivance known for propelling them but sails. When the bluecoats (that's the name they had in the countryside) heard of the wreck in the Island and of her cargo, they kept rushing into the Island night and day, without allowing themselves time for sleep, for they had a splendid boat, well-equipped, and they themselves were knowledgeable men. They worried the life out of the Islanders, who were trying to hide the lumps of palm-oil in holes in places where neither cat nor dog could come at them.

Anyhow the people lived very well in the Island that year, though the bluecoats did their very best. They took a lot of the palm-oil across Dingle Bay, and sold it on the opposite coast every night, though the bluecoats got away with enough of it to pay their rent, too. They came in on their boat one day, only four of them. An Island boat had just got in with six great lumps of the palm-oil in it. The coastguards took them into their boat at once, and they were very pleased with themselves. There was a young woman on the landing-place with a huge lump of jagged rock in her hands. She went into her father's boat, and the first thing the bluecoats knew was that she had flung the rock right through the bottom of their boat and the ocean was coming up through the hole. Out came the bluecoats. Out came the lumps of palm-oil afloat once more. The women brought them to shore again. The King's men had to drag their boat up the beach and patch her with a piece of tin, and once they had her put to rights, they made their best speed home. I fancy they didn't come visiting much more after that during all the palm-oil season.

Some time after that two of the men were on the hill and they saw a sheep that had fallen down on one of the beaches. They went down to recover the sheep, but, looking round, one of them saw a brass bolt under an over-hanging rock. He worked it out. It was four feet long. The whole beach was full of them—bolts of brass and copper. Nobody knows what quantity of that kind of metal the two of them salvaged that day, for that was the beach on which the ship had been wrecked, and great timbers from her were still there. The Islanders made a good deal of money out of the bolts that year.

Those were bad years, and if it hadn't been for that shipwreck, nobody would have survived on the Island, the old people used to say. I often heard with my own ears the old hag over the way saying that God Himself sent that ship amongst the poor. They lived well enough for a year or two because of her when the whole countryside on the mainland was famishing in extremity. When my father used to bring home a load of those bolts in a bag, it was beyond my strength to stand one of them on end. It's an ill wind that blows good to nobody, and our folk often got through a bad year with the help of storm and tempest, though it was a bad business for poor people who were at the mercy of the wind.

The day I first wore breeches I nearly went out of my senses: I was like a puppy dog unable to stand still. I felt no need to eat at all, and I didn't eat anything, either, but kept on running in and out, this way and that, and one of the family keeping an eye on me. Now, once when I came up to the fire, my mother looked at me and saw a patch of wet on my grey breeches. 'Heavens!' said she, 'that's what you've done, I'll bet.' I told her that it was so, and that I'd asked Nora to undo the buttons for me, and she hadn't done it. I suppose that was the first lie I ever told, for I hadn't asked Nora, though my mother gave her a good talking-to for not doing it. It's hard to be condemned for a crime you haven't committed, but see how soon roguery showed itself in my nature. My father set about the breeches again, for he was the one who had tailored them, and he made a smart job of them, so that they were ready for any use without trouble from that time out.

Eight years old I was that time, my mother said. Off I went visiting from house to house through the village next day, Eileen with me. It was the custom in those days, when a boy had a new garment or a new suit, for him to go into every house. You'd get a penny or two to put into your pocket in each house. I had three shillings in the pockets of the grey breeches when I came home. I gave them to my father, I remember, though I'd rather have given them to my mother, for she had more trouble with me than he had. But since my father was a smoker and, after all, he had made the breeches, I gave them to him.

Soon enough there was a hole through the bottom of the

breeches, with my shirt hanging out. My mother said that she must patch them before she went to bed. She did it, too, and warned me to take care and not make another hole in them again so quickly or I'd get a slash of the stick. I got it all right next morning!

It was a very fine day by the time I had a hen's egg down me and a cup of milk, and whatever else I had to go with them—potatoes, I suppose. I didn't escape the eye of the old woman across the way as I ate that meal. Her talk was changing now as she saw me growing in strength and spirits.

'My dear,' she would say to my mother, 'keep at him. He'll make a fine man yet.'

She was wrong in that, too, for nobody since has ever said that I was in any way kin to Oscar.

She was purring like a cat, to gain her own ends, for my father used to bring home all sorts of game, and her own man wasn't handy in that way at all. He was a fumbler on the hill and in the field, and good morsels were always coming her way in our house.

I was leaping out of my skin on the floor at that time, set up with myself, the grey breeches high and trim on me, full to the chin of food; and, if anybody felt the troubles of the world heavy on him at that time of day, it wasn't me.

As the height of the morning came on, I was sent off to the White Strand with Maura. When I reached the strand, I ran for all I was worth. Maura cast an eye along the strand and saw a school of porpoises rounding the Gob from the south, and they never stopped till they came over against us, just out from the shore, with their great fins sticking up out of the water, all of them close together like any shoal of fish. Maura had often seen them before swimming singly, but she'd never seen a great school of them like this. She thought that they would come ashore, and she was terrified. She took me on her back, and we hastened home.

When we got home my mother cried out that the boats were coming, and that some of them were making a ring round the porpoises, trying to drive them ashore. There were three large boats working seine nets in the Island in those days, and seven of them in Dunquin. Every one of those boats was on the scene busy about the porpoises, the Island boats trying to drive them ashore, while the crews of the Dunquin boats remained standing by, jeering at them. At last one of the porpoises went high and dry up on the strand. Some able fellow drew his blood, and when the rest of the porpoises smelt the blood they came ashore, helter-skelter, to join the other high and dry on the sand.

When the Dunquin boats saw the rich prey ashore and those on land drawing their blood, in they came to take boatloads of them home with them, but those on shore wouldn't let them take a single one. It wasn't long till the men there were as bloody as the porpoises, and the Islanders drove them down the strand covered with cuts and wounds. There was one Dunquin boat that never stirred hand or foot to interfere. The Islanders gave them the best porpoise on the strand, and the six other boats went home without a taste of them. Some of them found it hard enough to go at all. It was a tough job getting the porpoises home and salting them. But the people didn't spare their trouble, for in those days you could hardly get anybody to exchange a porpoise for a pig. My father's face was red with his own blood and the blood of the porpoises, but I knew him well enough all the same, for I had my wits about me then.

I jeered at the old woman whenever she came along with a creel full of porpoise meat balanced on her rump. You might imagine that she came out of one of the porpoises herself with her creel, she was so thickly smeared with blood. But she had earned a meed of praise, for she nearly killed the captain of one of the Dunquin boats with a blow of a shovel.

The Islanders had no lack of pork for a year and a day after that day, and it would have lasted two years if it hadn't been for all the relations they had everywhere on the mainland.

There was no risk of me forgetting that day even if I should live to be a hundred. Everybody you saw was crimson with blood instead of being pale or swarthy. Another thing, I was within an ace of being killed myself on the strand before any sea-pig or sea-bonham died, and Maura with me, if we had been so unlucky as to be caught in that skirmish with the porpoises on the shore.

The old woman took her food with us in the evening.

When I was a little lad, I used to hear tell of 'the wheat-ship'. That was another example of what storm on the sea would bring us and the help it would be to us when other people had suffered the limit of ill fortune. The year this ship was wrecked on the White Strand I can't remember, for I wasn't born or thought of in those days. But I know well all that happened to her, and all the people she saved from death in the famine time, and I can give an exact account of her fate—how all her crew were lost when she was cast upon the strand, and not a soul of them all could be saved. It was from the woman over the way and from my mother that I learnt my lesson, for they used to be chattering together often and often.

There wasn't a vestige of canvas on the ship except for one rag on the foremast. They had to run her ashore on the White Strand. She struck far out, for she was deeply loaded. The men on board tied a piece of timber to a rope's end, but they failed to come ashore. The people said that they had never seen a wilder day. The wind was blowing out to sea across the strand. At long last, a block of timber from the ship came ashore on the strand somewhere.

Those on shore and those on sea dragged on the rope, but, alas, it broke, and away went the sailors southward through the smother. The Islanders have been the worse for that sight ever since. A while after the ship split in two.

If she destroyed her own crew, thousands survived the worst year of the famine through her. Those thousands of sacks of wheat saved the Islanders, for they lasted them and their relations a long while. If it hadn't been for her, not a soul would have survived in the Island, and you may be sure that the old hag said that it was God who sent her to the poor.

Eileen was only a year old when the ship struck, and she's still alive in the New Land (i.e. America). Her contemporaries have had a pension for three years in this country; that makes her seventy-three. My mother was on the strand, though she was only six days up from childbed. Pats, my brother, was strong enough to be there, too, although he was more a trouble than a help there, for he hadn't wit enough to look after himself. A lot of things came ashore, though there was much that didn't, for the wind was offshore.

The wheat began to sift out of her, too, as soon as she split. I suppose that it wasn't in bags at all, but cast loosely into her like coal or salt, for they gathered it mostly at high tide. It was drifting in from time to time—so as to give the people a chance to save it, they used to tell one another. They had to wash it in water to take the salt out of it, and then spread it in the sun, and after that they dried it by the fire. Then they would boil it till it softened and turned to a thick mash. *Baighrean* the people called it. Whatever else came their way, that was a great stand-by to them to keep them alive. I used to hear the old hag saying to my mother, again and again, that she never lived better in her life than the time it lasted. She had a double row of teeth and two sets of jaws grinding together. It was said that she chewed the cud like a cow.

In the days when I wore the grey breeches, and went about on my own, I used to go to meet the boats every evening. The most common fish in those times was pilchard, and they were full of bones. They are very like herrings. The fishermen hadn't a good word to say for them. They're a small fish, and a lot of them go to a pound. Moreover, they rotted the nets. My father called me into the boat one evening, while they were throwing out the fish, and he put me behind him in the stern. I was peering about me, and before long I saw a line with a bit of pilchard on the hook. And what do you say if I didn't throw out the bait. My father saw me doing it, but he didn't trouble himself about me, for he never thought that there would be any fish so far inshore to take the bait.

But before long a fish bit, and I had the line twisted round my legs. The fish dragged me overboard. All the men on the harbour shouted out to my father, but, when he turned round, he saw his darling swimming away. He stuck the boathook into the grey breeches high up on my backside and dragged me into the stern of the boat. He pulled in the line, and it was as much as he could do to get the fish aboard. It was a huge big conger six feet long.

My greatest fear was that my mother would kill me for getting my breeches wet. The girls were bursting with laughter at me, but I wasn't grown up enough to have any feelings of pride. Stout young women they were in those days, up to their bellies unloading boats, as sturdy and strong as any girls that ever were in Ireland.

I went home hand-in-hand with Nora till we drew near the house, and then I struck and told Nora I wouldn't go a step farther, for my mother would kill me. She was coaxing me on, saying she wouldn't. By the greatest luck in the world my father came by, carrying a creel of fish. 'What do you want, Nora?' said he. 'Why don't you take him home? He's dripping wet.' 'He won't come with me,' she said. 'He's afraid of mother.' 'O, come on, Tom, my lad. It was my fault you got wet, for I called you into the boat,' said my father. He seized my hand, and off I went with him.

When I went in, I wasn't as lively and playful as usual. My mother saw that there was something up. She sat me down near the fire, for she thought that something else was wrong with me, and before long I had the hearthstone swimming wet. My father came in. 'Have you taken the clothes off him yet, for he's wet through?' he said. He was dragging the conger behind him. He brought it in, and it was as long as the hearth.

'Yerra, is it how he fell into the sea?' said she.

'Don't you see the fine big fish he caught? And for the first fish he ever caught, it's a very fine catch,' said my father.

He told her the whole tale then, and saved me. All my clothes were stripped off me and dry things put on me. I didn't like the breeches I got, for they were an old, patched pair. She didn't give me tea either, but a mug of porridge with milk, after all my swimming.

2. *My Schooldays*

THERE came a very fine day, a Sunday it was, and some
business brought in a big boat from Dunquin (nothing was
known of canoes in those days, or for some time to come).
When the boat reached the harbour, the people said that
there was a lady on board, but the lady turned out to be
a schoolmistress. When I heard that, I was anything but
pleased, for at that very time I was just beginning to go
hunting by myself on hill and strand, with nobody to keep
an eye on me now, for I was a big chap, they thought. I had
a little rod, with a hook hanging from the tip of it. Each
of us boys would have a score of minnows fished out of
holes, not much of a catch, but we kept pet gulls, and the
minnows were the very thing for them.

Well, Monday came, and when breakfast was over they
couldn't find the man with the grey breeches. The girls
were ready for school, but the hunter was to seek. Maura
was sent out to look for me, but she reported to my mother
that I was after minnows, with two other boys in my
company—Johnny Meg and Mike Peg.

'He can have to-day,' said my mother, 'but may
God take my soul to-morrow if he slips off without my
knowing.'

I came to my gully and gave him the minnows I had
caught. When I went into the house I wasn't so set up with
myself as I would be other days. I saw that my mother had
the net ready for me; besides, the old hag next door was in
before me to see the beating I was to get, for I used to be

mocking her unmercifully in those days. But my mother was too clever for her!

When the girls came home from school, my mother catechized them about the mistress, and asked what sort of woman was she—kind or cross. They all said she was a splendid woman, and that she didn't strike or thrash them. That's when my mother brought the talk round to me.

'Look at this fine fellow, running round all day since morning, in danger of tumbling head over heels into a pool, getting fish for his gully. But I'd have him know that he'd better be ready in the morning to go with you, in God's name.'

'Maybe,' says Kate, 'he'll play the same trick on you to-morrow, since you didn't frighten him.'

She was the pertest of them all, and the one I liked best.

'O, he'll be a good boy to-morrow, Kate. The beginning's always the worst,' said my mother.

We were on the best of terms with one another till bed-time came, the girls talking about the school, and telling my mother the teacher's name. But they couldn't bring out the name till late into the night, and they started to squabble together, so that I had as much fun over them as they had over me earlier on. At last Maura managed to get the name out—Nancy Donoghue. It was a difficult name for them, as they had never heard anything like it in the Island. Then off we all went to get ready for bed.

Next morning each one was ready for his post, and the meal was prepared pretty early, for—'the tide doesn't stay for high noon'.

Pats was in good trim in those days. He was the second oldest of the litter, only Maura was in front of him. My father was preparing ropes and a sickle for himself and Pats up and down the house. Maura and my mother were to go with them. It was flood-tide, and a fine day for cutting black seaweed for manure. Kate was to be the

housewife; Eileen, Nora, and I were for school—that's
how we were settled or arranged that day.

A potful of boiled potatoes, fish and milk with them, we
gobbled down our bellyful of them, young and old. As for
tea, nobody in the Island in those days had ever seen a
kettle, or for long after.

The horn blew, and off went the shore party, off went
the scholars.

Kate stayed at home, quite grown-up.

'Be a good boy at school, Tom, my lad,' said my mother;
and I thought she wouldn't leave a trace of skin or nose on
me, she gave them such a scrubbing before she went to the
shore.

I was ten years old that day I first went to school, my
mother told me—about the year 1866.

As I went into the schoolhouse, hand-in-hand with Nora,
I was bold and lively. Poor Nora thought I would make a
show of her, but I didn't. The teacher was in the doorway
and she gave me a fine apple, and I was surprised when I
went in that nobody else had one. But she didn't intend to
give us an apple every day—though I thought then that she
did! It was a handsel apple given to every scholar the first
day. This was my first day, and that's why I got it.

My prowess at school was little enough till I'd ground
down the apple. I had good grinders in those days, though
I can't say the same of them now.

I didn't take long to cast my eyes all round the house.
I saw books and papers in little heaps on every side. A
blackboard was hanging on the wall with white marks all
over it, made with chalk apparently. I was beside myself
with wonder what they meant until I saw the teacher
calling up the oldest girls to the blackboard and point out
the marks to them with the stick in her hand, and I heard
her talking some kind of gibberish to them.

I nudged Pats Micky, who was sitting by me on the

stool. He's the same Pats Micky who has been King over us now for a long while. I asked him in a whisper what was the rigmarole the teacher was talking to the girls round the blackboard.

'Damned if I know,' says he, 'but I fancy it's a sort of talk nobody will ever understand here.'

I thought that hunger would make an end of me at school, but bedad it wasn't so, for pretty soon the teacher spoke: 'Playtime,' says she.

The word made me stare, for I hadn't the faintest idea what it meant. But immediately I saw the whole crowd in the school jump up and rush out through the door. Nora had to take hold of my hand before I would move from the stool. We all of us ran home.

There was a handful of cold potatoes waiting for us. They were set down by the fire, and we had fish with them —salted scad, and that's a very sweet fish. My mother had brought a dish of limpets from the strand with her, for they had returned from it while we were at school. She was roasting the limpets and throwing them to us one by one like a hen with chickens. The three of us hadn't much to say, but were chewing away at the food till we were near to being full. My mother began to question me then about the school, for she was afraid I'd choke myself if I answered her with my mouth full.

'Well, Tom, my lad, isn't school fine?' says she. 'How did you like the lady?'

'O, the great big apple she gave him!' said Nora.

I was cross with Nora for not letting me answer her for myself.

'Did you have one, Tom?'

'I did, mom, but Nora took a bite of it, and so did Eileen.'

'But it was a great big apple,' said Eileen; 'we left enough for you.'

'Off with you again, my dear,' said my mother to me.

We spent some time more in school, and the King kept his seat on the stool at my side. He was a fine, easy-going lump of a lad, and so he was always. We were the same age. He'd often point his finger at some boy who was being naughty—screeching out, maybe, or a pair of them setting about one another with both hands, or a lout here and there with his nose running. Sights like that worried the King, and he used to point them out to me. See how the character that is born in a lad sticks to him throughout his life. That's how it was with the King when he was a child. He didn't care for such disgusting, vulgar sights; but as for the rest of them, it's little enough they troubled their heads about them. So it's little wonder that when knowledgeable people came our way and thought that there ought to be someone with the style of King in the Island, they chose out the man fit to take the title and to carry it with credit.

My day at school hadn't lasted long enough yet for me, and it was too early for me when the teacher called out: 'Home now!'

Some of them stuck in the doorway, they were so keen to be gone.

A slice of bread and a drink of milk were ready for us. There was always any amount of fish ready cooked, but often we hadn't any fancy for it. Pats used to have as good a catch as my father in those days, and there was plenty and to spare in the cabin for us, a marvellous fire, 'kitchen' enough to go with all sorts of food that came our way, to gulp down with an edge on our hunger.

Off to the strand we went for the rest of the day.

The next day the whole lot of us were for school, for the spring tide for seaweed cutting was gone.

I saw that my mother was wearing her new dress, and I wondered what was up. She ran across to me and took me by the hand, hung my clothes on me, and gave me a kiss.

'Be a good boy now,' she said, 'until I come home. I'll bring you some sweets from Dingle. Do what Maura and Kate tell you, and go to bed when they say.'

I began to cry, but not for long. I started off for school with Nora and Eileen. Maura and Kate stayed behind to look after the house because my mother was going out.

When we went in, the whole crowd was there, though my chum hadn't come yet, the one I liked best. Little books were being given out that day, new things were being written on the blackboard and the old ones rubbed out. Other big objects were hung up here and there on the wall. I gazed at every one of them.

I had finished examining them all when the King came in, and I was delighted to see him. His place was waiting for him and he made his way to the seat beside me, and from the way I saw him thrusting through the others, so as to be next to me, I realized that he was as fond of me as I was of him.

'I'm late,' said he in a whisper.

'Most of them have only just come in,' I said.

The teacher called us up to the blackboard. She explained the letters on it to us six times.

Friday came, and when the day was over and we were getting ready to go home, she told us not to come back till Monday. Most of them were delighted at this announcement, but I wasn't over-pleased, for I'd rather have come back, not from any passion for learning, I suppose, but because I liked being with my chum the King.

My mother wasn't due back from Dingle till Sunday, and Maura and Kate thought that they wouldn't get me to bed whatever they did, and they began to coax me and to be very nice to me. But before bedtime came at all I fell fast asleep on my father's knee, and he told them to take me to bed. They did it at once. It was the cock woke me in the morning, and it was high noon then. Since I hadn't lost them any sleep the night before they were all busy about me, all waiting on me. I wasn't quite the fool they imagined me to be, believe me. I had all my teeth and could use them to eat anything, and was further on than anyone would have thought at my age. For a proof of this, the old hag over the way had stopped calling me 'mother's darling' and 'old cow's calf'—all the things of the kind she used to say to my mother about me, though anybody would be ready to take his oath that the cow, whose calf she was, was fifty years old.

On Sunday my mother came home from the town. She had a white bag and a coarse cloth bag with her, and all sorts of things in them. But there wasn't a taste of sugar or tea among them, for nothing was known of them in those days. It was I who carried the white bag home, and I found it heavy enough, though its chief contents were clothes for the girls.

The grey old hag was waiting for me in the house to hear the news from Dingle.

The first thing my mother took out was a two-peaked cap, and she put it on my head.

'By the Virgin!' said my father, 'you've made a complete peeler of him!'—and all of them burst out laughing.

'Well, maybe he'll get a post yet,' said she. 'He's young, and learning's to be got in his day, and he can stay at school till he's picked up all there is there.'

How well I remember that speech, for the troubles of the world changed that tune.

She had apples, sweets, cakes, loaves, tobacco for my father, a pair of boots for Pats, white dresses for the girls, and a great deal more. The grey woman had a taste of everything, for she was a little woman who liked a bit of anything that was going.

School every day then for all of us, except Pats, who was a great big fellow now going out fishing with my father.

Maura didn't spend long at school either, for she was a woman by this time. There were four of us getting on very well, helping one another to learn.

One day, after we had been let out of school, we saw all the people in the village collected on the cliff above the harbour, and both the teacher and we wondered what was up. A boy peered across to Slea Head, looking intently.

'Holy Mary! look at the boats in the midst of the tempest and the smother,' said he.

The boats were given up for lost, and nobody thought that we should ever see any of the crews again. The Island boats had a boat adrift in tow and the sea was sweeping right over them. They reached the harbour at last, for the tide was with them, and that was a great help to them. The wrecked boat was a fine big one. The captain was in her with two other men and a young lad about sixteen years old at his last breath. They lifted him to land out of the boat, and he died immediately. He is buried in Castle Point—the place where Pierce Ferriter had his castle when he ruled here.

It was beyond the power of the whole Island to bring the wrecked boat to shore, and the great sea swept her away again. My father was in her, acting as captain. Alec was the name of the captain, a fine big man. The name is still remembered on the Island, and will be for some time, for there are many on the Island who were born the year the boat came. They got salvage for bringing them to land, and many of those who lodged them were well paid for it. We were using a saw my father got out of her till the other day.

My sister Maura was a fine vigorous woman by this time, and as there were three more of them, they arranged to find her a home in one of the other houses. The chief man in the Island at that time was Paddy Martin. He had ten milch cows for a long time, but I never saw that much in his possession, for he had two sons married in other houses, and he had given them some of the land, and cows, too, no doubt. He had five cows at this time, and his youngest son still lived at home unmarried—young Martin. A match was arranged between Maura and Martin, for what he wanted was a woman who knew what work was and was able to do it; and, in all truth, Maura was a woman of that kind, and I don't say it only because she was my sister. They didn't ask my father for any money, for they knew that he had none. They had had enough to do to keep us alive in difficult times.

Martin and his father and mother were all living in the house in those days, four of them, counting Maura, after the marriage.

Martin lived only a year after his marriage, and then my sister had to return home to her own people, for one of Martin's brothers came back to live with the old people. They wouldn't give Maura anything, although Martin left a boy child. Maura left the boy with us and went off to America. After three years there she came back home again. She had the law of them, and got the father's share for the son.

Soon afterwards the teacher was summoned home at Shrovetide to be married. That meant that the school was closed for a time until a thin lath of a master called Robert Smith came. He wasn't very nice to the rabble of scholars he found. My chum the King didn't like him at all. He had an unfriendly way with him. The King used to pretend to me that he came from Russia. A great mug he had on him, hollow eyes, and a sleek swarthy complexion. He had prominent teeth, and a bush dripping from his nose like a goat's beard. But the bush wasn't the worst part of him, for it was fair in colour and hid his ugliest feature.

The mistress married in a village in Ballyferriter parish. Her husband was a blacksmith, and the parish priest favoured him, I suppose. She got a school in that place, and spent her life there till she got a teacher's pension. They are in the grave now, after eighty years of life, every one of them. That was the end of the first school-teacher that ever came to the Blasket.

Before long all the boys were whistling at Robert, and the girls laughing, and I tell you there were great lumps of women at school at that time. Robert soon saw that he would never be able to do anything with them. He spent only three months among us, and off he went.

As I was crunching my bite of food one morning, I was looking about me on this side and on that. My mother came in at the door with a sharp piece of iron in her hand —a piece of a boat's grappling. She didn't sit down, but set about looking for something else. She found a bag in the search. I was watching her like a cat watching a mouse, for I knew that she meant to go down to the strand.

'Well,' said she, 'would any of you like to go down to the strand, the day is so fine?'

It has always been a custom here to go and get 'kitchen' from the strand to eat on Good Friday for anyone who has the opportunity.

'Sure, mom, I'll go with you,' said I, jumping up from the table, though I hadn't finished my meal.

'Of course you can, but finish your meal, my love. I'll wait for you,' said she.

'I'll go with you, too,' said Nora.

'So will I,' said Eileen.

'There's nothing to stop you,' said my mother, 'since the world has been so good to you as to close the school.'

My father and Pats were digging in the field, Kate was looking after the house—with the baby in her charge, for Maura was over in the States. My mother charged Kate not to think of anything else in the world but him till she came back.

We went out at the door and turned our faces to the strand, and I was beside myself for joy, if any of them was, I was so set on paddling in the sea in my grey breeches. When we reached the strand there wasn't a single rock that hadn't a woman or child of some sort picking limpets and winkles, and such-like seafruit of every kind, that came in their way.

It was the ebb of a spring tide, and to the west of the strand there was an island called Woman's Island that could only be reached at a very low tide: limpets and winkles were very plentiful there because they were never gathered. It was separated from the nearer shore by a deep channel, but there wasn't much water in it that day. Before long I saw my mother gathering her skirts together and bringing them forward between her legs. I didn't mind a bit that the world should see my mother's legs and calves, for there was nothing stunted or lumpy about her: she was a fine well-grown woman, fair-skinned and bright from crown to heel. My grief is that I don't take after her in my whole person. But I suppose what ruined me was that I was 'an old cow's calf', for the rest of the litter were good-looking enough. I was watching her carefully to see what she meant to do. She called out immediately to the women near her to go to the Island with her. Four of them responded at once—the old hag over the way, my aunt, White Joan, and 'Ventry'. The water was above their knees, but a wash upset my aunt and Ventry and tumbled them head over heels. Ventry gripped my aunt very neatly, and they set them on their feet again. Anybody would take his oath that the old hag and my aunt came of the same parents; they had the same complexion, the same height, and the same way with them.

I was snivelling—my mother was so long out of sight. Nora kept egging me on, but Eileen was trying to stop me. Nora was always very much down on me, and we never could get on together. But I understood the reason of it when I began to grasp things, and the old hag used to give me a hint of it, for, often enough, we'd just as soon be fratching as praying. Nora had been the favourite for five years before I came. I came unexpectedly, and, when they saw me, Nora's nose was put out of joint. And that's the reason why she thought less of me than the others did.

Before long women here and there began calling out that the women on the Island were cut off by the tide in the channel. Not a soul of them was to be seen. Off went everybody to look at the channel. The tide was flowing, and there was a man's depth in the channel already, and that was the moment that they came into view, every woman of them with a full bag. They had to stay where they were. Everybody present said that they'd have to stick there till morning, and I was beside myself when I heard it.

Some of the girls on the strand ran off to carry the news to the men on the fields that the women were cut off by the tide on the Island. Most of the men faced for the strand, but my father ran to the house to get a ladder. Very soon I saw him coming towards me with a ladder, twenty feet long, on his shoulder. They laid it so as to reach across the channel, but it was too heavy to put in the proper place. My poor father had to take to the water and swim across to catch hold of the end of the ladder, and fix it in a crevice in the rock. My mother was the first of them to go across on the ladder. Ventry followed her, and they came to land splendidly. Then the three others ventured on it. Two of them were on one side of it, and the third on the other side, so that the ladder overbalanced and upset, and down they went into the sea.

I was in high spirits now I'd got my mother again, singing 'Donal na Greine'. But I changed my tune soon enough, for my father had to jump into the sea again and bring his sister to land on this side, and take a grip of White Joan; and the old hag over the way was going under when he caught her by the hair. I was at my last breath by the time my father landed: the old hag very nearly pulled him under as he tried to save her with her apron full of limpets.

3. *Our Houses*

THEIR DESIGN · THEIR FURNITURE · OUR
ANIMALS AND FOWLS · OUR FOOD AND DRINK

I MAY as well give some brief account here of the way we managed things in this Island when I was young, more particularly since the fashion of that world has passed away and nobody now living remembers it except a few old people.

As for the houses that we had in my youth, and for some time after, they differed among themselves, just as in other places. Some of them had a handsomer appearance than the rest, and others were pretty wretched. A number of them were only ten feet by eight. Others were larger—from that size to fifteen or twenty feet long. To divide the house into two a dresser stood out from the wall in the middle of the floor, and a partition met it from the other side. There were two beds in the lower portion, where people slept. Potatoes would be stored under these beds. A great chest was kept between the two beds up against the gable end. On the other side of the partition —the kitchen side—the family used to spend the whole day, or part of the day, ten of them perhaps. There was a coop against the partition with hens in it, and a broody hen just by it in an old cooking pot. At night-time there would be a cow or two, calf or two, the ass, the dog on a chain by the wall or running about the house. In a house with a large family you would find a post-bed, or maybe a bed on the floor. The old people used to spend the night in that beside the fire, with an old stump of a clay pipe going, or two pipes if there were two of them living, and smoking away; they would have a wisp of straw for a pipe-lighter,

A good fire of fine turf smouldered away till morning; every time they woke they took a light from the fire and puffed at the pipe. If the old woman was alive, the old man would stretch across to give her a light from the wisp; then the smoke from the two old pipes would drift up the chimney, and you could imagine that the couple's bed was a steamship as they puffed away in full blast.

Two or three dogs would stretch out at the foot of the bed, the cow or the cows below them, head to the wall, and there would be a calf or two with the run of the kitchen, or lying muzzle to the fire. The ass would be tied up on the other side of the house opposite the cows, and a cat with a couple of kittens, maybe, in the chimney niche. The rest of the trumpery in the house was stuffed under the post-bed for the night. This bed was more than a couple of feet from the ground, and it was made of wood or iron. Some of the houses had no division to make a room, but there was a post-bed in one corner and a bed on the floor in the other. The dresser was up against the wall or the gable-end. Every kind of house had two or three barrels of fish. And, besides all the other animals, you would find a pet lamb or two running about the house.

Those houses were made of stones mortared with clay, and most of them were very roughly finished, for their building was always hurried through, and everybody took a hand in it. Rushes or reeds were the thatch, over a layer of thick and stout scraws. The thatch would have been all right if the hens would only have let it alone, but they wouldn't. As soon as the rushes began to decay, and worms could be found in them, a man with a gun couldn't have kept the hens away from scratching and nesting there. Then the drips would begin, and a dirty drip it was too, for there was too much soot mixed with it. The hens nested so deep in the thatch that the women often lost them, for a hen wouldn't even answer the call to food when she was broody. The little lasses very often brought a hatful or a capful of eggs down from the houses. The children made a mess of the thatch, too, always hunting for eggs. It was as good as a day at Puck Fair to listen to two of the women whose houses adjoined, quarrelling with one another about the ownership of the eggs.

The good houses were from ten to twelve feet wide, and from twenty to twenty-five feet long. They had a cupboard and a dresser arranged crosswise to make a room of the lower half of the house, and two high post-beds below them. They were thatched in the same way as the little houses, though the hens had an easier job with the little houses, because they were built lower. I remember, however, a funny thing that happened in one of the big houses, the like of which never occurred in one of the little ones, in this very matter of hens. The family of this house were gathered, every one of them, round the table at supper, with plenty of potatoes, fish, and milk before them, and all their jaws keen set to grind them and send them on down. The man of the house was sitting at the head of the table, with a wooden mug full of milk beside him. He'd just put his hand to his plate, to take out a piece of fish, when he saw some object fall into the mug. He looked down, and there was a lump of something drowning in the milk. They had to fetch the tongs to get it out, and not a one of them had the faintest idea what it was.

'It's a young chicken,' said the woman of the house, 'whatever the dickens brought it there?'

'It doesn't matter a damn to you what it is,' said the man of the house. 'It has sent you out of your wits soon enough,' said he, 'for where on earth do you imagine a thing of that kind could come in your way from?'

All at the table were getting madder, and Heaven knows how the evening would have ended if another chicken hadn't fallen on the potatoes, alive and kicking.

'For God's sake, where are they coming from?' said the woman of the house.

'Can't you see that they're not coming from hell, anyhow,' said the man of the house. 'It's some consolation that they're falling from above.'

A lad at the lower end of the table glanced up at the timbers of the roof and saw the wind and the sun coming through.

'Devil take it! there's a hole in the house,' says he to his father. 'Come here and you'll see it.'

When the man of the house saw the hole, 'Wisha,' said he, 'may Satan sweep all the hens and eggs and chickens out to sea.'

'God turn a deaf ear to you,' said the wife.

When they went to the hole to close it, they found ten other chickens and the hen.

I was cradled in one of the medium-sized houses. It was a little cramped house, but what there was of it was kept neat, for my father was a very handy man, and my mother never knew what it was to be idle. She had a spinning-wheel for wool and another for flax, and combs for carding, and she used to have the job of spinning threads ready for the tailor with the distaff from her own wheel. Often enough she would spin it for the other clumsy women who couldn't put themselves in shape to do it, and were too lazy, anyhow, even if they knew the trick.

Some ten years after my marriage I built a new house. Nobody handed so much as a stone or a lump of mortar to me all the time I was at work on it, and I roofed it myself. It isn't a large house, but, all the same, if King George were to spend a month's holiday in it, it isn't from the ugliness of the house that he would take his death. It is roofed with felt, as every other house and shed in the village was until the Board put up six slate-roofed houses. When the new house was finished, a hen fluttered up on to the roof. My uncle Diarmid was just going by. He stopped tó watch the hen and the desperate struggle she was making to maintain herself on the roof, but the slippery felt shot her off.

'Devil mend you,' said my uncle, 'that the day has come upon you when the roof shot you over the cliff!'

In my young days Patrick Keane, and some time before him, Patrick Guiheen, were the two chief men in the Island. I remember when this Patrick Keane—the grandfather of the King we have now—had four or five milch cows. I never saw the other, Guiheen: his grandchildren were alive in my day. I've often heard that he had eight or ten milch cows, a mare, and a wooden plough. A red mare she was. She helped to draw the gravel for the old tower on the Island, whenever that was built, and he was in attendance on her when he was sixteen years old. John Dunlevy, the poet, was a baby in the cradle at that time. That makes the poet sixteen years younger than the King's grandfather. The men of their standing had some half-dozen houses that were pretty good.

The tables used in the little houses were rather like a kneading trough—a board with a raised frame round it to keep in the potatoes or anything else they put on them, and a stand of tripod shape that could be folded up so that the stand and the kneading trough could be hung up on the wall till they were needed.

One day my uncle Liam came back from the strand with a fierce hunger on him. The tripod frame was standing ready, with the kneading trough on it, full of potatoes and whatever 'kitchen' went with them. A good-sized potato fell from the trough. Off went the dog after it. He carried the stand away with him, and the trough and all its contents rolled every way through the house. His wife fell to gathering up the potatoes. 'Holy Mary! little woman, it's as good as a fair day with you,' says Liam.

We had bowls and plates in every house, wooden mugs, a chair or two, and a few stools. The chairs had seats of twisted rope made of hay or straw. There was a pot-rack of iron in every house, and still is, to hang things on over the fire, and there was a pair of tongs of some sort or other on the hearth.

They have cups and saucers in every house now and a full dresser, making a fine show. Only human beings live in the houses in these days; the animals have their own sheds out-of-doors. Cressets and fish-oil, with tapers or rushes on the cresset, renewed as they burnt away—that's the first contrivance for making light that I knew. The fish-oil was got from scad and pollock. 'Dip' was the name we gave to the scad's fat; the pollock grease was called 'liver'. We used to melt it. They employed seal-oil for light, too, but they didn't put much of that in the cressets, for they used to gulp it down themselves, dipping their bread of Indian meal in it, and they needed it badly enough. I was well in the teens, I think, while this kind of light was still in use. The cresset was a little vessel, shaped like a boat or canoe, with one or two pointed ends, three or four feet to it, and a little handle or grip sticking out of its side—the whole thing about eight or ten inches long. The fish- or seal-oil was put into it, the reed or wick was dipped in the oil and passed over the pointed end of the cresset, and as it burnt away, it was pushed out. The pith of the rush formed the wick, and often they used a soft twine of cotton or linen for it. They would often use a large shell instead of a cresset for a light. I don't remember at what date paraffin came in. A fragment of turf or a chip of bog-deal was the older fashion, I used to hear them say.

I lived for a long time from my young days on two meals a day. I'd have a lot of work done on strand or hill or in the field, and the cows would be coming to milking when I'd be thinking about taking my morning meal. The sun would be far down in the west when I had the evening meal. We never called them breakfast or supper, but always the morning and the evening meal.

Potatoes and fish and a drop of milk—if there was any—that was our food in those days. When the potatoes failed, there would be only Indian meal, just shelled. People to-day couldn't make a shift to eat the bread it made, do what they would; they haven't got the teeth for it. I am sorry that I don't have the same food to-day, with the same jaws to eat it with, and the same good health.

In the days when I was young two stones of flour used to come in every Christmas. I was a grown man before tea was known, and, when a pound of tea came our way for Christmas, it was sparingly used, and the remnant saved up till the next Christmas. But the tune has changed altogether in the matter of food for a long time now. We have wheat-flour in these days, and tea and sugar. Some of them fiddle with food four times a day. At that time we used to eat as much food in one meal as in those four meals put together. People lasted two days on one meal of the kind, if they needed to. A man can't go a pike's length in these days without tumbling on his backside, for they don't eat a meal at all, but a miserable bite or two.

4. *In School and Out*

THE FAMILY OVER THE WAY · A NEW TEACHER
COMES · THE CRABS · THE FOUR-EYED INSPECTOR

THERE was only a yard between us and the house over the
way, and both houses had only one door apiece. The other
family had the lower half of the yard and we the upper,
and the two doors faced one another. If the old hag had
wanted to, she could have scalded my mother from her
own doorway with boiling water, and my mother could
have done as much to her. My mother often bade me keep
clear of the grey woman, for she had a cranky nature, and
she herself had to purchase peace from her, and that was
true. Still she had a generous heart.

My mother used to do everything for her, for she was an
untidy worker, and so was the man she had—my father
used to tighten up everything for him, spade and ass gear,
even the thatch on his roof. I never saw a man more
unhandy at his work than he, but he was a thoroughly
decent man. Bald, or Crop-eared, Tom they called him,
for he hadn't a button's breadth of ear on him. But he had
the brains of the seven seers in his head, so that, if he only
had had the education, he could easily have bested the
whole of Ireland. My mother often sent me to him to find
out when such and such a holy day was due, and if they
were eating any manner of food, the two of them would
come between me and the door to force me to take some
of it. I never knew a more hospitable cabin, and since it has
come to pass that all who lived in it in my time are with
the company of the dead, and I live still, may God grant
them a better habitation than that poor wretched hut.

They had a son and a daughter. I don't know whether
there were ever any other children. The daughter had her

mother's wild hair, and the son was a stunted, spiritless loon, and he had his father's untidiness. The sea never suited him. He'd no sooner set foot in a boat than he'd be seized with violent vomiting. So he never brought back a catch from the sea, and he spent much of his time as a labourer.

There was nobody living in the Island, young or old, or in the mainland parishes either, that Bald Tom didn't know his exact age—the day, the year, and the hour of his birth. The people said that there wasn't his like for a long memory in the countryside, though he didn't know the ABC in any language. He often used to tell me that the Christmas cakes were ready baked when I was born, on St. Thomas's Day, that comes three days before Christmas— that was the day my mother found me on the White Strand. 'How many years ago is it now?' the grey woman would ask. He never hesitated: 'Fourteen years ago come Christmas,' he would answer.

From that time on the old hag used to be making up to me, for my house made me the messenger between the two houses. I took more from my house than I brought back to it. I'm not making a boast of it. Maybe it wouldn't have been so if there had been plenty in the other house.

I remember one Sunday, when every lass and lad faced for the White Strand, every one of them carrying a hurley, and after a meal, not of bread, but of potatoes. Soon I was ready, too, my clothes well buttoned up, new clean breeches of undressed sheep's wool, my policeman's cap with the two peaks, and my face dipped into a basin of water and scrubbed clean. It wasn't my mother who washed me in those days, for I was a man grown, my boyo!

I started for the strand with my hurley—a furze stick with a twist in the end of it. Nora and Eileen went with me, and we went straight ahead till we were in the middle

of the hurly-burly, and not a one of them on the strand
wore shoe or stocking. Those days of hurling on the strand
on Sundays were the hardest days any of the young people
had to face.

Somebody spied a boat coming from Dunquin under
full sail, and when she was making the harbour we'all left
the strand and went to meet her. There was a woman in
the stern, the new teacher, a sister of the first one, Kate
Donoghue, a fine, comely girl.

School again on Monday, you may be sure, and we were
all of us at our posts. Sure enough the King found his place
next to me. As I was ten years old when I went to school
for the first time (1866) I must have been fourteen at that
time—that is, in the year 1870. The teacher had new little
books to distribute. She kept the blackboard going, too,
and she was amazed that there was hardly anything she
put on the board that one or other of us couldn't explain,
so she had to make it harder. The Island children took
great delight in this new employ, and, that being so, they
had a natural gift for learning. Some of us had the spirit
of a King: all of them had the spirit of the sea and the
great ocean in them. The breeze blowing from the shore
was in their ears every morning of their lives, scouring their
brains and driving the dust out of their skulls. Though I
had a King in the making to sit by me whom the hammers
of a smelting mill couldn't drive from my side—whatever
it was that made him take interest in me—he kept me from
going ahead, for he was always glancing restlessly this way
and that. That's the chief fault I had to find with him, for
he was always distracting me just when I was beginning to
make some progress. We got on very well, but we were
always glad to see Saturday come to set us free to go
romping off wherever we wanted.

Well I remember one of those Saturdays after St.
Patrick's Day. It was a fine, calm year, and there was a

dearth of fish in the village just then. My father came in at the door, after working in the field, and there wasn't a bite of food ready for him. 'What's brought *you* home?' said my mother to him. 'It's a lovely calm day,' says he. 'If I could get a crab, I might have the luck to catch a string of rockfish,' and out he went again.

What do you think if I didn't go out after him, and when he saw me coming after him, 'Where are you going?' says he. 'I'll go with you,' said I, 'and look after any crabs you catch.' He went eastwards past the landing-place, and out to an island there. He had to swim across. He dipped his head under water and brought up two crabs from one hole.

He brought them to where I was standing and gave them to me to keep—a male and female crab. The names we give to two crabs in one hole are *collach* and *fuaisceán*. Collach is the word for the male crab, and he hadn't been long in my hands before his claws separated, and when they closed again he caught me by the thumb and the next finger to it, and I couldn't shift or shake him off. I screamed like anything for terror, and my father heard me at once. He came running to where I was, for he knew well enough why I had screamed. The crab had me in so tight a grip that my father was forced to break its claw off, and even then he couldn't get the claw apart without smashing it with a stone.

Well, there were my two fingers useless, and the worst of it was, it was my right hand. My blood was sprinkled on the ground and my fingers as black as coal, but my father didn't mind so long as I hadn't fainted—though I was near enough to it. He twisted his hat-lining round the fingers. He expected that my mother would be angry with him for letting me go with him, but she wasn't. My sisters were very sorry when they saw the state I was in at the end of the day. My mother plunged my hand in hot water and washed it carefully. That did it a great deal of good. Then she got a plaster and bound it up. The pain left it then.

I was singing 'Donal na Greine' at once. The grey woman came in to ask after me. If she was an old gossip, she didn't want me to lose my fingers. I'll take care to give her her due, since I can't explain my own life without bringing her in again and again, for I never got a sight of the sky any morning in the year without seeing her, too.

My father had four crabs. He thrust them into a bag and went off along the hill, a good way back, to find the likeliest places. He was away the length of a tide and more, and he didn't come back empty-handed. He had a bagful of fine speckled rockfish, and when my mother emptied them out there was a heap of them. She took up a big one and turned to me with it. 'Here, Tom, my lad, be off with this one to the grey woman.'

I didn't say no to my mother, even if I'd been unwilling —and I wasn't. Off I went with the rockfish, and handed it to the old hag. She wondered where I had got it, for she didn't know yet that my father had caught anything. She liked me well enough by this time, though there had been times when we weren't the best of friends. She began to be so sweet to me that you'd have thought that I was a little god to her. Bald Tom, her husband, was at home, and the daughter and the son, too. They'd just finished their morning meal.

'Have you got anything to give him?' said Bald Tom.

'I've nothing that he hasn't got already,' said she, 'but I'll give him this girl for a wife when he's two years older.'

Although she couldn't have promised to give me anything more precious to her than the fruit of her own womb, I felt at once that that promise would bring me more harm than good.

The speckled rockfish and the old hag's speech plunged

me into despair, and no wonder, when you think of the gift I was to get when two years were up.

The new teacher spent three more years with us before she caught her sister's complaint—a marriage proposal. Her people came from the neighbourhood of Dingle, and a lad from the town married her—a pleasant, personable man.

We were in school one day when a boat came from Dunquin. A watch was kept for all the boats coming in, for unpleasant people were about in those days—drivers and bailiffs watching to snatch everything they could lay their hands on, and leave you to die of hunger.

But the man in the boat that day was a school inspector, and not one of that kidney. When we heard that, we were in a bad way. A lad kept going to the door to see when he would come in sight. A bouncer of a girl saw him first. She dashed back from the door with a look of horror in her eyes. Soon enough he entered the house. You could see a child here and there with his hand over his mouth, and, as for the big girls, one of them burst out laughing, and pretty soon another one joined her. The inspector had his head in the air staring, now at the wall, now at the timbers of the roof, and now at the school children.

'Holy Mary!' said the King to me in a whisper, 'he's got four eyes!'

'He has,' said I, 'and a light to match in them.'

'I've never seen a man like him,' said he.

Whenever he turned his head, there was a glitter in his eyes. At last the whole crowd burst out laughing—all the big ones, and the young ones were screeching for fear. The teacher nearly fainted with shame, and the inspector was beside himself with rage.

'There'll be murder done,' said the King again under his breath to me. 'I wonder now did anyone ever see another man with four eyes?'

That was the first person wearing spectacles that the children ever saw.

The inspector gave the teacher a good talking-to, in a jargon that neither I nor anyone else in the school understood, and when he'd finished his speech, he seized his bag and went out of the door, and on board the boat that was waiting for him, and never came back to the Blasket again.

This madman left the school as he found it, without putting a question to a single child, and I'm ready to make a bet with my readers that they've never read of a similar case, nor will as long as they live. The poor mistress fainted as soon as he'd gone. I had to go and fetch a cup of fresh water for her. Eileen sent me to the next house for it.

We had full leave to talk before the teacher recovered.

'We'd better run off home,' said the King to me, 'while she's weak, for she'll surely kill us when she comes to herself.'

'Yerra, there isn't much of a soldier in your make. What a funk you're in!' said I. 'Wait a bit and we'll get what the others get.'

In round about half an hour's time she came to. All of us thought that she'd leather us as long as there was any warmth in our bodies, but things are not always as you expect, and so it was this time. She didn't strike a blow or speak a sharp word to any of us. She could have dealt with the case of one or two, but, since we were all in the same boat, she treated us sensibly—a thing she couldn't have done if she hadn't possessed sense. She sent us home at once, and she had as sore need as any of us to get back to her own house.

The King was as fascinated as any of the scholars by the sight of four eyes in one man's head, but he never said as the others did—that the man came from hell.

A month or two later another inspector came to us: a lean, swarthy, withered man, but he had only two eyes in his head. He fell to work and asked us all searching, difficult questions. There were eight in my class. One or two of them rose high and tall above the others. Though all of them had fine handsome heads, and the inspector thought that such heads must hold the answer to every question, that wasn't the way of it at all, for the little skulls put them to rout. The inspector was in the brightest of humours when he left. He gave a shilling to the best scholar in each class, and when he handed out the shilling to our class, it wasn't one of the big ones that got it, but myself. My father was delighted when I gave it to him. He got a fine lump of tobacco out of the inspector, though it wasn't only the inspector that brought it to him, for if I'd failed in class, it wouldn't have come his way.

5. *My First Visit to Dingle*

IN A BOAT ON THE SEA · THE VIEW ON
LAND · JERRY SEASICK · DINGLE · THE NEW SHOES

IT was holiday-time with us for a while after that, and it
was a fine calm year. The big boats were bringing home
quantities of fish. The three of them were full to the brim
every day. As my father and Pats had two men's share, we
always had a fine show of fish in the little house.

That was the first time, I think, that I ceased to be a
spoilt darling, for my sides were sore that day from carrying the fish home in a bag on my back. Each man of the
crew had a thousand fish, so that made two thousand for
us. My father said that I carried more than a thousand
home. 'And I'll take you to Dingle with me to-morrow,
if the day's fine,' said he, 'for the boat's going to fetch
salt.'

When I heard that I could have cleared a house with
one leap.

It wasn't me, but Kate, that was first to look out at the
door next morning, for she was my mother's help at that
time. She was too big and too old when the school came.
I saw her right enough.

'How's the day, Kate?' said I.

'Very fine,' said she.

I was at her side on the hearth at one bound.

'Holy Mary! what's got you up so early, or what are you
after?' said she.

My father was the next to get up, and he put on his
new clothes. He looked out at the door. Then he told Kate
to give me my new togs. She didn't know till then what
I was after.

My father took a bagful of rabbits' skins, and off he

went to the harbour. The others came along, one by one, as they were ready, till the whole boat's crew was collected. They came about the boat on either side, and thrust her down till she was afloat on the main sea. The oars and sails were put aboard, and then they set her prow to sea and her stern to land, as they did in the old tales long ago.

Two sails were run up, and we had a good helping wind east along Dingle Bay. Another lad of my own age was in her, a cousin of mine named Jerry. By the time the boat was east of Slea Head, Jerry was changing colour till he was as white as paper. The men knew well enough what was the cause of his change of colour, but I hadn't the least idea. I thought he was on the verge of death. His father came to look at him, and told him that if he could be sick, he'd be all right. The boat was running along very sweetly now, for she had wind and to spare. Soon one of the men said that Jerry was being sick. He was, too, poor chap, and all the food he'd swallowed that morning was thrown overboard to feed the gulls. I was bursting with laughter, and Jerry was crying.

An uncle of mine was at the helm, and I kept putting questions to him, asking about every strange thing I saw. There was a big slate-roofed house in the middle of a farm. 'Who lived or lives in that house?' I asked.

'A pretty bad person,' said he, 'Bess Rice. Have you ever heard tell of her?'

'I've often heard my father, and Bald Tom, too, talk of her,' said I.

When we came in sight of the fine, broad harbour of Ventry, we could see a lot of big, white houses. He named every one of them—the Catholic church and the Protestant church, the police barracks, and the coastguard houses, and everything else that took my fancy.

My companion was coming to himself now that the gulls had snapped up all the contents of his belly; his voice was a feeble, famished squeak, and he had a worn, deathly look. He came over to where I was with the steersman, who was his uncle, too.

'How far is it to Dingle Harbour?' he asked the captain.

'By my cloak! it's a fair way yet, my good lad,' said he, 'and I think you'll never get there alive, since you've nothing left in you but your guts. Sure you're not a bit like the other lad.'

The words had hardly left his lips when the men saw a fierce squall of wind, and they had to pull down the stern sail, and the boat hardly managed to carry the foresail—the sea whitened so under the wind.

She was not long after that in making the mouth of the harbour. I thought at first there was no harbour there at all until we'd got half-way in, it was so narrow, but after a bit it widened splendidly till it looked like a lake.

We reached the quay, and my eyes were as big as two mugs with wonder. I saw gentlefolk standing there with chains across their bellies, poor people half-clad, cripples here and there on every side, and a blind man with his guide. Three great ships lay alongside the quay, laden with goods from overseas—yellow grain in one of them, timber in another, and coal in the third.

Before long my father called to me, saying that all was in readiness, and that the men were going up to the town. Off we went, I and the boy Jerry, and, though there was little enough remaining in his body after the passage, he would rather have been left looking at the ships than attend to the call to food. All the crew of the boat, big and little, crowded into one house. There was a table laid with bread and tea for us, and I promise you there was little said till we were near to being full fed. They paid the woman of the house, and out they all went.

The salt shop was the next place they went to. Every man had his own bag with him. Two hundredweight of salt was put in each bag, and we left the salt there till we should be ready to go back.

I followed my father then into all the shops, and, though Jerry's father was there, too, he stuck close to my heels. The pockets of the grey breeches were not empty of money that day. When the boat was ready to start on the return journey, my father searched my pockets, and, as most of their contents was copper, there was a good heap there. When he had finished reckoning up, 'By the breviary!' said he, 'you're only a shilling short of the price of a pair of boots.'

Who should be present at that moment but a sister of his, a woman who was always in Dingle—now at home and now in the town. 'If that's so,' said she, 'here's the shilling, too, for you, and put the boots on him, since this is the first time he ever came to town.'

When I heard my aunt say that, my heart leapt for joy, for I knew well that my father wouldn't go back on his word. I was right.

'Come along then, we can get them just up there.'

Off I went with him, wild with delight. I had no stockings to put on my feet, but the woman in the shop gave me some stockings on condition that my father should bring them back again. It's then that my boots squeaked under me. It's then that I felt a gentleman. And who dared say that I wasn't! A suit of undressed wool on me and a two-peaked cap! Jerry was cheerful enough till he saw the new boots on me, but he hadn't a word to say after that.

When the boat reached the landing-place in the Island, loaded with salt and food from Dingle, according to the custom which we still have to-day in the Island, the cliff above the creek was crammed with people, be sure, to see if there was any news. There was nobody in the boat that they didn't recognise at a glance but the young gentleman

—some of them maintained that he was a child of great people in Dingle who were sending him to spend a week running about the Island. One of my sisters, Eileen, was among them on the cliff, and she couldn't be certain that it was me because of the shining glory about my feet, for I was a thin-legged, barefooted starveling when I left home. Kate and Nora were at the boat down by the water. Pats, my brother, carried the bag with two hundredweight of salt home on his back, for some of the fish was still unsalted.

My mother thought some great finished man was coming when she heard me pounding along with my pair of boots. Everybody marvelled at my getting boots so soon, for in those days men and women alike didn't usually put on boots until their wedding day.

The two of us who had been in Dingle were served with a three-cornered lump of bread and a saucepan of milk. We didn't care for fish; we were sick of it. Nora jumped up and brought four eggs.

'I thought,' said my mother, 'that there wasn't an egg in the house to-day.'

'I found a hen's nest on the roof yesterday with eight eggs in it,' said she.

'You'd wait long enough before you found a hen's nest, or a cock's nest either, on the roof of a slated house,' said old-fashioned Kate.

When I'd devoured my lump of yellow bread and my saucepan of milk and my two eggs, out I went, and lost no time in going straight into the old hag's house to have a bit of fun with her, for I was as deft a speaker as herself by this time. The poor woman welcomed me home from Dingle. 'May you live to wear out your boots; how soon they've put them on you!' said she.

When I saw how courteously she treated me, I put my hand in my pocket and gave her an apple. I gave them all an apple, and sweets, too, for my mother had charged me to do it. She sprang up, crunching the apple like a horse chewing, and took half a rabbit out of the pot and handed it to me.

'Perhaps you'd fancy that,' said she, 'since you're such a man.'

'But I can't eat it,' said I.

'Give it to your mother, then,' said she.

I took the rabbit home with me and handed it to my mother. She gave me a leg of it, and I picked it.

Night was coming on, and very soon I began to nod and went to bed. I fell dead asleep at once, for I was weary after my visit to the town.

It was school time and past next morning when I jumped out of bed. My mother told me that I had almost died in my sleep. I was as lively as a trout then, however. I plunged my head into a basin of water and rubbed the sleep out of my eyes, and off I ran to school.

6. *Bald Tom and the Old Days*

THE King was in his usual place, and, being big and heavy, must have left his mark on the stool. He was whispering to me about Dingle. He'd been there himself—three times, once with his grandfather, and the other times with his father. But it was 'sweets' that were at the bottom of his blarney. I knew that well enough, and I should have been a poor friend, too, if I had forgotten him. I handed four to him, and he was very grateful.

We were let out in the middle of the day.

'Listen,' said the King. 'The mistress will be leaving us soon.'

'How do you know?' said I.

'She got a proposal yesterday. She is to be married at once.'

'What sort of a man is he?'

'A gentleman's coachman somewhere.'

He was right, for she only spent the week with us, and went out on Sunday. The school was shut again.

It was about 1873 that the second mistress left us. That meant I was sixteen. I had had six years at school, and I hadn't mastered English or near it.

On Monday—since there was no school—the King ran in to me pretty early in the morning. He had had his breakfast, too, and I was just beginning mine. I was eating a fine fresh loaf of new yellow bread, just taken from the fire, and 'since it's a rare thing to see a cat with a saddle on him', as the old saying goes about any improbable thing, I had a lump of butter, too. We had a good milch cow, and my mother had made a lot of butter in a big tin. I had a salted scad and a saucepan of milk, and, better than all, a mill of teeth to grind them with.

My mother was pressing a hunk of bread and some butter on the King, but he wouldn't take it. Probably he hadn't much appetite left that morning. My mother would never have offered the yellow bread to him, if he had been called 'King' in those days, but he wasn't.

The King's business with me was to take me fishing from the rocks if we could get a crab for bait.

'Take care of yourselves,' said my mother, 'when you're after the crabs, for it's neap-tide.'

Out of the door we went to hunt for crabs, but we had no luck at all.

'There's nothing in these little holes,' said the King. 'We'd better take our clothes off and go under the water in some place where we're likely to get them.'

No sooner said than we were stripped to the pelt and diving under and coming up again both of us. I went into a hole as deep as myself, and when I got my foot into the hole there was a crab there. It was hard for me, and more than I liked, to get my head down as far as my feet, but it was harder still to let go the thing I wanted. I bent down, but the water kept me up, and I couldn't get my hand to the crab. I thrust my foot down into the hole again, and what do you think! I fetched him up on one of my big toes. He was a huge male crab, and, usually, if one of those is in a hole, his mate is along with him. I put my foot down again and found the other one, but it was a smaller one than the first, and came easily. I had enough bait for the day then.

The King came to me with his clothes all buttoned up.

'Come along,' said he, 'we've got plenty of bait for the day. You have two fine crabs, and so have I.'

ISLAND KITCHEN

I dressed, and off we went along the rocks. The King had to go back to the upper village, for he wanted a line and hooks. But he was with me again at once. We went westwards to Dunlevy's Point, named after the Island poet. Rockfish were biting freely, and every now and again we pulled up a fine fish and put it behind us. At last I was throwing out my line, and if the hook didn't catch in my finger! I'd caught my last fish that day! The King had to cut the twine that bound the hook to the line with his knife. The hook was fixed in my finger with the twine hanging from it. I didn't feel much pain, as the hook wasn't very far in. We had forty rockfish—twenty apiece. The King carried them all home, and we divided them in our house. The hook was taken out at once, for Kate cut away the piece of skin in which it was fixed with the razor. My finger gave me a lot of pain, and I suffered a good deal before I was through with it.

Bald Tom used to spend every night with us till bed-time. He was excellent company, and I hardly noticed my sore finger most of the time when he would be talking and telling tales of the hard times he had known. Though my father was much the same age, he hadn't half his gift for remembering the past and recalling every detail.

'I wonder,' said my father one night, 'what the trouble was that set the parishes of Dunquin and Ballyferriter by the ears for so long in those days?'

'O,' said Bald Tom, 'haven't you heard the tale of the Boat of Gortadoo?'

'I have, indeed,' said my father, 'but I don't remember it very well now.'

'There was a ship adrift north of Beginish and a Dunquin boat went out to her. They boarded the ship and threw down into the boat everything they fancied. A boat set out from Gortadoo with twenty-one men in her—the chief men in the parish. They never stayed till they came up to the drifting ship. On board they went, looking for booty and laying their hands on things already picked out by the Dunquin people. They came to blows and had at one another, and the Dunquin men were driven from the ship. The Ballyferriter crew were throwing things out of the ship till their boat became overloaded and sank, and every soul in her was lost except the last two, who remained on board throwing the things down, and they never came out of her.'

'Perhaps those two are still alive in her,' said I to Bald Tom.

'Hush, you whelp,' said he. 'That ship was smashed to atoms against Ferriter's Raven that very afternoon.'

'And how did it come,' my father asked Bald Tom again, 'that the people of the northern parish were so bitter against the Dunquin folk for so long after?'

'Yerra, my friend,' said Tomás, 'because they didn't take a single one of them out of the sea, though they were beseeching them, and gripping the blades of the oars, praying them to take them in, but all they did was to drag the oars out of their grasp and leave them to go with the tide.'

'And wasn't it strange that they didn't save some of them, though their boat could hardly carry all the twenty-one in addition to her own crew,' said my father.

'It wasn't possible for them to take them all,' said Bald Tom, 'and they weren't keen to do it either, seeing that they had attacked them in the ship and had taken out of their boat anything they needed or had a fancy for, and had refused to let them come near the ship once they themselves were on the scene.'

'I suppose,' said my father, 'that the two crews were related to one another.'

'They were,' said Tomás, 'some of them very closely, and that nearly caused the wreck of the Dunquin boat, for one man tried to drag on board a relation of his who was clinging to an oar-blade. But the captain put a stop to that, saying: "They'll all be trying, one after another, to save their own relations, and the boat would never manage it." So the twenty-one from the Gortadoo boat were drowned and the Dunquin boat came safe home with all her crew.'

'I expect the people of the northern parish were savage with them,' said my father to Tom.

'Yerra, man,' said Tom, 'they were laying for them at church and at the fair. Didn't they come over in the dead of night? They used to go into the houses and maltreat the people in them. They killed a fine young fellow, the son of a woman of my kin, in the mill of Belaha, out there on the mainland, and every market-day in Dingle there would be six or seven in need of a priest after the day's brawls.'

'And what made peace between them in the end?' said my father.

'I'll tell you that,' said Tom. 'A girl from the cantankerous crowd wedded a Dunquin man—that was the first peace between them. But it was a long time before that came to pass—after they'd half-killed one another!'

'God bless the souls of the dead!' said my mother. 'I never heard a proper account of their doings until to-day. They were a merciless, savage lot in those days. Thanks be to God, again and again, that that world is passed away!'

It was getting near bedtime and Tom was thinking of going home and the rest of our family coming back from visiting in the cottages.

I spent a month suffering from my finger, with little pleasure or merriment. But it never felt sore or painful while Tom was telling his tales. He used to be in our house every night, and, as my father said the rosary every Sunday, Tom repeated it every Sunday with us, and he was a great hand at reciting his decade.

Tom was poor always, and he had to put his son out to service in Ballyferriter. He spent five years herding cattle there, without a shoe or a stocking to his foot. Not long after the son went, the passage-money for America came for the daughter from an uncle of hers on the mother's side. She went off at once and spent five years there. They had to fetch the son home then. The girl sent a pound or two across the water now and again that was very useful to them.

The old hag over the way was often up very early in the morning after her daughter went away, and she was often heard keening in the dawn. There was nothing strange in that, for the girl was all she had, and she never looked to see her again. Every time I heard her keening, I felt very sorry for her.

One morning that she was out early, what should she see riding off the harbour and the White Strand but a steamship at anchor, full of dark men—that is, men with dark clothes and caps. She rushed off in a panic and knocked at our door.

'Donal,' she cried.

'Hullo!' said my father. He thought that there was something up with her son or with Tom himself.

'What's wrong with you?' he asked.

'There's a big ship anchored out in the bay just below your house, full of men with dark uniforms and high caps.'

'That's so,' said my father. 'It was due to come sooner or later, and I fancy there won't be many houses left in this Island by evening.'

'God's everlasting help to us!' cried she. 'The news is always getting worse, but we never touched bottom till it came to losing our huts.'

We were all up in a second and off to the landing-place.

When I came on the scene the women gave me a job. I was set to gathering stones with the rest of them. We never rested till we had a ship's load of them heaped up. One of the women said that they surely had enough ammunition now, and that something would have happened by the time we'd shot it all off. 'But I expect,' said another woman, 'that the bullets will have killed us all first.'

'Yerra! may you die as they died in the Doon! Won't you be better off dead than lying in a ditch, thrown out of your cabin?'

A big boat crammed with men put out from the ship's side, and when they came inshore they were astounded to see the vast gathering above the harbour. They had expected that every living soul would have hidden in terror. And no wonder! for every one of them had a gun ready in his hand. But these women weren't a bit afraid of them.

The men went off and the women gathered round, every one of them with a chunk of rock in her hand. The men in the boat didn't know what to make of it when they saw the women standing their ground, and they slowed up as they came in to shore. At last they ran the nose of the boat on the rock, two of them standing in the prow with nothing to do but keep their guns levelled at anybody who should lift a hand against them. As soon as the first man left the boat, a woman flung a great stone down that came near to knocking him off his feet. He glanced up at the cliff and pointed his gun at them, but not a woman stirred. They kept their ranks unbroken above the harbour. Soon a woman threw another stone, and then another, and another, till they made the whole beach echo with the clatter. No more men got out of the boat, but they had to make haste and take the man they had put on land aboard again, and clear off out to sea as hard as they could. Two other boats coming in met them, and they held a consultation. Then those boats drove into the creek in a furious rage. They ran the stern of their boats hastily on the rock and landed their men; but all the same the stones showered down on them, and one of their men was struck on the crown of his head and laid out flat at their feet. It was a light stone, for one of the little lasses had flung it. He'd have been a dead corpse if it had been one of the strong women who had thrown it!

The captains commanded them to get back into the boats at once. They did so—though they were delayed by having to take the half-dead man with them. The three boats, full of armed men, stood by for a time to talk it over, and the result of the talk was that they came to make another attempt, for they thought that the women had shot off all their ammunition. But the boys had gathered another pile of stones, and they began to cast them down again, and, though there was a danger that the armed men might fire on the women, they weren't a bit afraid. They felt less fear than they inspired.

There were five women standing to one side, and they hadn't enough stones to throw. One of them was carrying a fat lump of a boy in her arms, and think how angry or frantic she must have been when she couldn't find anything else in her neighbourhood to throw at the two police who were trying to make their way up a grassy slope below —'Devil take my heart,' said she, 'I'll fling the child at them!'

'Yerra, you cursed fool,' said the woman next to her, 'don't lose your wits; stick to the child.'

She had swung the child to throw it when the other woman gripped it. In that moment a woman had come up on the other side and flung a lump of sod down that sent the two tumbling over. The child that was so nearly thrown is strong and well over in America to-day.

The ship cleared off with all its crew that day without taking a copper penny with them.

When the report got abroad that a steamship had been in the Great Blasket with armed men aboard, and that they had failed to get either rent or tax, it set all Ireland wondering. Things stayed quiet for some time. A few years later another ship of the same kind moored below the houses. There were some civilian people in her and a few men with guns. The Islanders had been warned that something of the kind was coming, and that the best thing they could do, probably, was to let them have their way and to drive all the cattle and sheep to the western end of the Island. So they did. The lads drove them as far as they could. The sheriff was in the ship with all his officers. They were not interfered with, but the Islanders gave them rope to do their business. Off they went up the hill, the bailiffs and the police in a bunch. The sheriff went as far as the Tower and found nothing. He sent a number of them half-way across the Island, but it was just the same. They found two old mules with nothing alive in them but their eyes. The sheriff was asked if he wanted to take the mules with him. He wouldn't take them, for he was afraid that the people would make a joke of him, he said. They went home as they came—without cow, horse, or sheep.

One cold winter's night Bald Tom strolled into our house, as was his way. There was a great fire of turf blazing up the chimney, and, as the house was a small one, it was hot enough indoors, however cold it was without. The crop-eared man had come before I had time to get clear of the house. The other young people had gone visiting: that was an old custom, and our young people keep it up still. 'If you had any sense,' said my mother, 'you'd stay at home and not be off to those bare houses without fire and warmth, and you'll have plenty of entertainment with your father and Bald Tom,' said she.

It wasn't this advice from my mother that was the chief check on me, but I was passionately fond of Tom's tales, and that's why I chose to stay and listen to him. The first thing the two began to talk about was the ship on fire.

'Well, Tom,' said my father, 'we had to sweat pretty hard that day when the ship was on fire.'

'We had,' said Tom. 'Two of our crew nearly died when they stopped rowing.'

'We might have known,' said my father, 'since the ship was moving, that there was something driving her and that she wasn't on fire at all, as there was no wind and she had no sails up, and we were following in our boats rowing our guts to catch her, without getting any nearer.'

'That was the first steamship to come this way, and we thought she was on fire, so off we went after her,' said Tom. 'She was going to Limerick with Indian grain.'

'Boats came out from Dunquin and Ballyferriter as she went north,' said my father.

'Was it long after that that the fat bullocks came ashore?' asked my father.

'Just a year after, in the spring, a week before St. Patrick's Day,' said Tom.

'Weren't there a lot of them washed ashore, perfectly whole?' said my father.

'Nobody knows how many,' said Tom. 'There were twelve barrels of salted meat in a single house in Fearann in Ballyferriter parish.'

'We made least out of them, I think,' said my father.

'Yes, and there was a reason for that—the weather was stormy and the men couldn't go out to fetch salt. But, however ill provided they were, the man that had least got a year's meat. I had more than a year's supply, though I went shortest of all, as I had no salt. I fancy you had enough of it to pay your rent, Donal?'

'I had four barrels, brim-full, cured and salted,' said my father. 'That was a great year for potatoes, and fish, too.'

'Every man in our boat made thirty pounds,' said Tom.

'Wasn't it in one of those years that the *Nora Creena* came, Tom?'

'The year after. Not a single pound was made that year, for the rascals in the old hulk seized every fish in the Island, and I've no doubt that somebody's curse fell on them when the bottom dropped out of the ship at Edge Rock as she was going back to Dingle full of fish!'

'O! the curse of everybody in the Island was on them, I fancy,' said my father.

'It was,' said Tom, 'and God's curse, too, and it fell on them all right.'

'How do you make that out?' said the other. 'You know not a soul of them was drowned when the bottom dropped out of their old tub. What was it saved them?'

'A great big boat they had tied to her, and when the water came spouting up they all went into her,' said Tom.

'But how else did God's curse fall on them, then?' said my father.

'Like this,' said Bald Tom. 'Some forty of them came to this Island in the days of the persecution to collect rent, and not one of them died in his own house except one man who lived out there in Coumeenole. They all died in want in the poorhouse; and that was only just. Thanks be to God that they are all dead and we are alive still.'

'John Hussey was the first honest man that came to collect the rent,' said my father.

'And a very straight man he was, too,' said Tom. 'He never took a penny too much off any man from the first day that he got the job.'

'That's true, Tom, but he often made trouble enough for people doing work for him. Boats had to go with him to cut seaweed and gather mussels for manure and to shear sheep without pay, and on bad food—a lump of yellow bread three days old and a mug of thin sour milk with the cream gone from it two days ago. And since the people survived him, and he didn't drown them, their luck will be in for good.'

'O! the curse of the twenty-four men rest on him!' said the small-eared man. 'He came near to losing a boat that I was in, rowing north through the tide with a load of black weed to Keel Harbour. The tide was too strong and the boat too deep in the water, but two good men in her threw overboard five or six horse-loads of the weed.'

'He took two boats' crews of us to Inishvickillaun to shear sheep,' said my father. 'We spent three days shearing them. The man in charge of the rock had brought some wreckage ashore, and we had to take the wreckage east to Beal Dearg.'

I never noticed the night slipping by as I listened to the two of them talking things over after this fashion.

7. *My Last School*

THE OLD SOLDIER AS TEACHER · THE INSPECTOR
COMES TO SEE HIM · MYSELF AS A TEACHER ·
HUNTING RABBITS

ONE fine Sunday a boat came in from the land with
strangers in it. Nobody knew who they were, and the
people gathered above the harbour. It was a big, lanky,
lean fellow, with a sickly aspect. He looked old, too. He
was married and had his wife with him and two children.
The woman had three legs—a working leg, a short one,
and a wooden leg. People began to snigger on this side and
on that, and someone said:

'They may be pretty miserable, but look what fine
children they have.'

'That's the will of God, man,' said another man,
answering him—a man who knew the points of the Faith
better.

They reached the schoolhouse. That house was divided
into two, to lodge the teachers. The people brought them
plenty of turf, and they settled in to begin their work. He
was an old soldier who had stopped a bullet or two in the
Army, and he had sixpence a day pension. He couldn't
lace up his boots or stoop at all because of the bullet in his
thigh. They were a wretched pair, not that I'm throwing it
up against them; but the three-legged woman was a bit the
better of the two, for she'd get to the town quicker than any
two-legged woman, for she stepped along fine with her
stick.

The school had been closed nearly a year at this time,
and it was opened on the Monday. Nobody was absent that
day. A new teacher, you know! The old people could
hardly keep themselves from going to see how the new

man got on. School-teachers were few and far between in
those days, and the priest hadn't been able to find anybody, and, as he thought the school had been closed too
long, he sent this man in for a while. He had never been in
any college and hadn't done too well in the elementary
school, either. However, study began in the morning on
Monday.

The King was waiting for me on his stool exact to the
minute. He beckoned to me to sit next to him, and I did
so. He whispered to me:

'Hasn't the old chap got a pitted skin?'

'He's pretty well pocked,' said I. My father had told me
that they were the marks of smallpox, but at that time of
his life the King didn't know what smallpox was at all.

The rabble at school didn't acquire much learning that
day, for they weren't attending to papers or books, but
staring at the three-legged woman, who showed herself
now and again. The teacher was a decent man, and we
weren't as frightened of him as we should have been of a
bad-tempered man. Anyhow the scholars behaved very
well with him.

Once a quarter he used to go to the town and bring
back a box of sweets and some apples to the scholars. If a
child stayed at home any day, he would go to visit him
with an apple or a sweet, and the child would go with him
gladly, crunching a lump of an apple like a horse. He had
such a kind way with him that few of the children missed
a day of school.

This was the last teacher I had, and the King, too, and
a lot of others, for he spent a good time in the Island. It was
ill health that drove him out at last. He started for Cork,
but he died on the way, poor fellow, near Tralee. There
was little learning in him that we hadn't picked up before
he went.

Though the master had a lean, swarthy countenance,

you would have thought that it wasn't the same man at all one day that an inspector came in at the door. There was a slight flush in his face such as you would see in a man who wasn't quite right in his head, and I'm inclined to think he was a bit that way then, whatever else was troubling him. I certainly didn't blame him for the change that came over him when the fellow entered, for the whole crowd in the school shuddered at the sight of him. He had such a thick, yellow hide on him that you would have imagined that he was cradled in some part of China. Every one of us, little and big, had nothing to say and went on quietly with whatever work we were doing. Before long the master came up to me with some figures on a slate and told me to cast them up as quick as I could. That was a soft job for me, and I soon had it done. The inspector had set him the task, and he was so confused that he couldn't make the sum out at all.

As the teacher was in bad health, the fright the inspector gave him made him ill, though the school was open every day. He said that he would be eternally grateful to me if I would take his place in the school, with the King to help me. His wife was a dressmaker, and she came to my mother and told her to say a word in my ear and urge me to take the school so long as the master was ill. 'And if you have a quilt or anything else to make, I'll make it for you,' said she.

The King and I were a couple of teachers for a month, and—keep it dark—we were a pretty poor couple, for, whatever we might have done, the misfortune and the mischief kept us from doing it. There were a lot of sturdy young things in the Blasket school in those days, and they paid more attention to playing pranks and courting than to making themselves experts in learning. Anyhow we got through the month in this fashion, free of all trouble and care.

Soon after that the teacher died. The school was shut up again and the King and I were together once more, free to follow the chase on hill or sea. If I had a touch of the spoilt child in me still because I was the last of the litter, the King was the same way, because he was the first of the litter. For that reason we were free to do almost anything we liked, good or ill.

One morning he came to me very early.

'You had some reason for coming so early,' said my mother to him.

'We'll go hunting,' said he. 'It's a very fine day. We'll run from here to Black Head, and maybe we'll get half a dozen rabbits. Where's Tom? Asleep still, I expect.'

'That's just what he is,' said she.

'Here I am, my lad,' said I, for I knew his voice better than the voice of any of the visitors to our house.

'Jump up and we'll be off hunting,' said he.

'But I've nothing any good for hunting with,' says I.

'We have, my boy,' said he. 'I'll bring the ferret with me.'

'But I'm afraid they won't let you have her,' said I.

'I'll steal her from my grand-dad.'

My mother gave me my breakfast, and I wasn't long gulping it down, and what I couldn't take at a gulp, I had a good mill to grind it down with—a slab of bread made of coarse Indian meal, hard enough for a horse, a scad, and water mixed with milk.

Off we went, the two of us. He stuffed the ferret down his chest. We had two good dogs, and I carried a spade on my shoulder. We made up the hill at our best pace. When we came near the rabbits, we found a warren. The King pulled out his ferret, tied a string to her and sent her in. Then he stretched a net over each of the holes in the warren. Soon a rabbit rushed out and the net caught him at once. That settled him, for there was a running cord to it that made a pocket of it.

He picked him out of the net, and set it again as it had been before. That was no sooner done than another rabbit dashed out at another hole. The ferret didn't come back till she'd sent out the last of them to us. The ferrets always come out when they can't find any more. Seven fine rabbits had been hunted out of the hole to us by the ferret and caught in the nets. Off we went to another hunting ground some distance away. The King sent the ferret in, and she stayed in a bit before anything came out. At last a big strong rabbit dashed out through the hole. The net caught him, but he pulled up the peg that held it, and off he went down the hill, but our two dogs soon caught him up.

When the evening was growing late and the sun sinking westwards, the King spoke:

'We'll never be able to carry the rabbits home for hunger,' said he.

'I never saw a man of so strong a make as you so quickly overcome by hunger as you always are,' said I, 'and if we don't get any more, I'll carry the lot home.'

We'd killed a dozen and a half by this time—a fair load—and we were thinking of turning our faces homewards. I had a coat with a big inside pocket and a large hunk of bread in the pocket. It wasn't I that put it there, but my mother. She thought, I suppose, that the day is so long and young people have good appetites, and she was right, too.

I pulled it out, tore it in two, and gave half to the King. Kings weren't as hard to satisfy in those days as they are to-day. He crunched it down with great satisfaction, and it tasted good to him, for there wasn't enough of it for him. When he'd chewed it all up, he felt himself strong again, and he put the ferret into one hole after another till we had a dozen rabbits apiece when we came home with the stars shining over us.

8. *Marriage*

My sister Kate married and went to live in a little house in the village. Her husband was a good fisherman. I often held him down under water with an oar whenever we wanted crabs for bait. I kept him under too long one day. He was at his last breath when he came to the surface, and his face was blue. He never trusted himself to me again.

The house Kate went to was just like the one she left— with eggs in the roof, too. Pats Heamish was her husband's name, for his father was called Big James. Pats had a fancy for joining the Army before he married, but his father used to say to him: 'Pats, my boy, think of the load on top of you!'—reminding him that he'd have to carry a bit of a burden. When the country people used to brawl and fight at the markets and fairs, Big James was captain of one of the factions, for he came from Ballyferriter to this Island. They were good enough at rough work, but they weren't handy. Kate used to climb on to the roof after the hens' nests there, for she had the trick of it, and would just as soon look for them there as in the coop.

I must leave them now to rub along together till my story brings me back to them again.

My brother Pats married the year after Kate. His wife was a girl from Dunquin, a weaver's daughter. They had two boys by the time she died. The youngest was only three months old and my mother had to set about bringing him up when she'd finished with her own clutch. Maura was still in America, and Nora and Eileen were at home. Maura meant to stay across the water till the other two

joined her, and so it fell out, for in a very short time she
sent them the passage-money. They went off in the same
year. As soon as she saw that they had their eyes open in
the New World, she began to think of moving, for her boy
was still in Ireland, and she wanted to get his rights for
him, and her own rights too, and to have the law of the
uncle who had turned them out. She reached the Blasket
at the end of harvest, having nearly a hundred pounds
with her. No sooner had she reached home than she set
the law in motion, and by the time she'd done with the
uncle—her husband's brother—he wasn't worth much.
She got something herself, and the money that was
adjudged to the son was put in the bank. Before long the
bee stung her, and she began to think of marrying again.
A tight young fellow, stout and strong, was the man she
chose, with nothing in the world but his clothes, and they
not too good. They built a tiny little new house for themselves and jogged along like anybody else. The young
fellow was a good fisherman, and, as for her, she could live
where a rabbit could—like all the rest who had seen
America or spent any time there.

Not long afterwards the bee stung my brother Pats, and
before anybody knew where he was, he was half-way across
to America, leaving the two young ones to my mother.
My father was well on in years, and there was nobody left
now for them to count on to keep the little house going but
the spoilt child—myself.

You see how soon we were scattered! The merriment,
the jokes, the fun that never ceased—before meals, at
meals, and after meals—it was all gone now, and not a
sound was to be heard but the voice of the old hag
opposite and the droning of Bald Tom: but, 'it was some
comfort that even they were there', as the man said of
Cuan Croumha.

'Wisha, God's blessing on the souls of your dead!' said

my mother to Tom one night. 'Have you the tale to tell of the hunters from the Island who were taken to Belfast?'

'That's a strange question to ask me, considering that my father was mixed up in that affair,' said Tom.

'Wisha, God bless you!' said she.

'He was, I tell you. He spent a fortnight away from home in misery. I was a little chap in those days, but I remember perfectly that I couldn't believe it was my own father when he came back. There was a boat's crew of them that went as far back along the Island as the Mullach Rour one fine, sunny day in a boat to hunt rabbits. They left the boat in a creek there and went after the rabbits on the hill. Before long they saw a ship coming through the Sound from the north, and she looked as though there was something wrong with her. They hurried down to their boat and went on board; and they'd have done better to stay where they were. It appears that the captain had a very short crew. He was a thorough rascal, and looked it. No sooner had they left their boat and gone on deck than he seized a gun and pointed it at them. He flung the Island-boat's rope into the sea and let her go with the tide, and prevented them from getting into the boat to go home. He forced them to hoist all his sails for him, and the night blew up into a violent gale. He carried them as far as the north of Ireland—as far as he was going himself, and if he'd been going farther, he would have taken them farther, too.

'He lodged them in an inn there, and ordered the hostess to have them there when he came back or she'd hear about it. One of them left the others by stealth—Big James's father—and no man that ever travelled through Ireland suffered as he did, without a shoe to his foot or any clothes to speak of, but hunger and cold vexing him and terror on the top of that, he was so afraid of being arrested from moment to moment. When the captain was ready he had them charged in court and condemned. They didn't understand what was going on, and nobody understood them, for they had no English, only Dunlevy's father knew a word or two. They would have gone to jail if it hadn't been for a gentleman who stood their friend. He heard all the talk going on as he passed the court-house, and he asked a youngster in the doorway what all the row was about. He told him what it was and where the men had come from. The gentleman was a captain in the Army, a native of Kerry. He went in at once to where they were, and, with the gentleman's help, the whole truth about the villainous captain was explained to the judge. He was condemned to pay down forty pounds on the table and the value of the boat he'd destroyed, ten pounds more.

'The man who had started out first was forced to walk all the way from the north, and he wasn't worth much when he reached the Island. He was a poor man with a large family, and, once the fear was upon him, he had no choice but to bolt as soon as he got the chance. I often heard my father say that the whole lot of them would have done as he did if it hadn't been that they agreed among themselves that their only chance of escape was to stand fast, though the captain would have been just as pleased if they'd all gone off. Although he told the landlady to keep them fast when he was speaking in front of them, he told her a different story behind their backs: to let them go if they showed any sign of escaping, for all he wanted was to get off paying them any wages; and he came very near to winning the trick.'

'Wisha, long life to you!' said my mother, who had been listening to the tale as eagerly as anybody.

Before we knew, Pats came in at the door, back from America, with nothing but his clothes, and poor clothes at that. I fancy somebody else had lent him the money to buy even them. We expected that he'd stay to keep us company for the rest of his life, but expectations are often disappointed, and that's how it was with Pats. The very next spring came a call from across the water for himself and his two children. He answered the call at once. He took up the little one, who could only just walk, in his arms, and kept him there till he got across. The other boy was strong enough. Pats started in to pay their way and his own, working hard every day, and he spent ten years thus. After all those years, though he'd never had so much as a headache or missed a single day's work, he hadn't saved a single pound. He was a tall, spare man, who had a passion for work, and he could do as much work as two men. That's the reason he was never in want of work for a day all the time he was in America. Of course, men were unemployed often enough in that period of time, but the ganger used to keep the best man to the last, and that was always Pats's lot.

Three of the family were at home now and three overseas. The old pair had to look to the pet now when there were only the three of us in the cabin. I was a good twenty years old at this time, and we did very well for some time. I used always to do marketing in Dingle, going sometimes by land and sometimes through the whole length of Dingle Bay. Occasionally we had pigs with us, or fish, or sheep, and so on, and now and again a bullock or a load of wool. On my first visits there I used to surprise the other men when I named the houses, for the sign outside told me who lived there.

I was in Dingle one day with Pats Heamish, my sister's husband, and we kept together all day long. He was the sort of man that couldn't keep a glass of whisky or a pint of porter long between his hands without pouring them down him, and he never enjoyed the taste of anything he paid for with his own money, but liked it well when another man jogged him in the back to have one with him.

The upshot of it all was that the drink got the upper hand of him entirely that day and made a complete scatterbrain of him. It didn't leave a stim of sense in him any more than he had on the day he first began to crawl after leaving the cradle. And since I hadn't had the luck to leave him before he went right out of his mind, I couldn't clear out now and leave him under the horses' bellies. Late in the evening we were in Main Street. There were crowds of people sauntering up and down, and some of them would come up to us now and then, acquaintances of ours, to welcome us in from the Island. He turned nasty at last.

'Where's this gang of devils from?' he kept saying. 'Talk's the best part of you. It isn't as easy to get a drink out of you. And your poor friends here parched with thirst!'

Sure enough he was telling the truth, but what was the good! The truth itself is bitter sometimes. It gave me a stitch in the heart to listen to his pointless babble, but what could I do but keep it to myself. Every now and then a brace of peelers would come our way, and I'd cheer up, thinking that they'd take him by the ear and relieve me of him, and put him safe somewhere till he recovered his senses. But so long as he saw them in the neighbourhood you'd take your oath that he was a parish clerk, he'd behave himself so well till they were clean out of sight. But the moment the King's men had cleared off, up would go his hat in the air and he'd be the merriest man in the street again. Some fellow would come up and let on to fetch him a clout, but Pats would give him a kiss.

Well, things were very well and not so bad; and bad as a man's case is sometimes, things can be worse often enough, and oddly though I spent the day with the rascal, the worst of all was yet to come. He shoved his hand in his pocket and pulled out his pipe, with its clay bowl, and nothing in it but chalk.

'Holy Mary! I haven't a thread of tobaccy,' said he. 'Come into this big shop here—they've got good tobaccy.'

'Yerra, we can get good tobaccy in the shops on our way home,' said I to him. 'Don't trouble about this one.'

'If I was there I should be coming back here after the good tobaccy they keep in this shop,' said he.

There's not a living soul that would say that he had a drop of drink in his body while he was jabbering about the tobacco. I knew that he wouldn't listen to a word I said, and off we went across the street. The big shop was a branch of a company from another part—Atkins's—selling all sorts of goods. It was a fine, handsome shop. There was a model of a woman standing on a chair between the two counters facing the doorway, as bulky as any woman of the countryside. When my man was coming through the door, he swept off his hat in greeting to the woman!

'Good day, Mrs. Atkins!' says he.

Ever since the days of the great famine no speech has caused so much laughter in Dingle as that. There wasn't a man from anywhere in the shop that didn't drop stone-dead, every one of them, writhing with laughter, shopmen and masters alike, when they heard what the fool said. If there had been the faintest trace of too much drink on him, none of them would have given a thought to what a man in that state said or did; but he showed no sign of it.

Night was coming down on us by this time, and the rest of the Islanders in the town were making their best speed home, but it was no good telling him that; he would sooner have gone east than west, and, in fact, that's the way he should have gone, for it was the way to the mad-house, and that was the best place for him that day.

When we left the big shop they were lighting the lamps, and we hadn't gone far when he said:

'I can't go any farther, Tom,' says he.

'Yerra, what's wrong with you now?'

'I'm dropping with hunger, and I'm thirsty, too.'

'Sure I thought nobody suffered from the two plagues at once.'

'Well, 'pon my soul, I've got them both now!'

I carried him off with me to a place where we could get something to eat. I thought they hadn't enough food for him in the house, but they had. What he ate wouldn't have kept a rat going. He went to bed, and nobody knew whether he was alive or dead till ten o'clock next morning.

When I got back home, after three days away because of Pats Heamish—Pats, the devil's own (God forgive me for calling him that)—there was a lot of wreckage afloat round the Island—all sorts of flotsam, timber and huge boxes full to the brim. Nobody recognised the stuff in the boxes when they broke them open. They kept breaking them up and carrying them home after throwing away all their contents.

When the Islanders saw that they could make no use of the goods in the boxes, they let the sea carry them past when anything else came their way. The women wore black flannel petticoats in those days, and they used to dye them with woad. They used to dip them first before they put the dark dye-stuff on them, and, only think! one of the housewives who had two petticoats to dip, got the idea of using the stuff in one of these boxes her husband brought for the first dipping. She had noticed that a colour came out of the stuff when it was damped. When once she had the idea, she carried it out, and it was a complete success, for no colouring matter ever went so deep into a petticoat as that did. She showed what she had done to one woman after another, and she'd no cause to be ashamed, for she had done the trick properly.

'What a godforsaken man I have!' said a railing woman who saw the petticoats prepared for the dye. 'He never brought a grain of it to the house for me, and I have had

two petticoats in the house for three months with nothing
to ready them for dyeing. I wouldn't give much for him
when once I get my hands on him.'

'For heaven's sake,' says the other woman to her, 'let
him alone.'

The woman hadn't been home long when her man came
down from the hill carrying a huge sack of turf.

'Devil take it, Joan! I've strained every sinew in my
back,' says he. He thought that she would sympathize with
him, you see, but she did the other thing.

'Sorrow on the day, I wish it had put your thigh out!'
says she. 'For it's a long day before you'd bring a richer
sack than that to my kitchen.' And her eyes were blazing
as she said it.

'Yerra, I can't remember when I left outside any sack
that was worth bringing home,' says he.

'Yerra, you devil, didn't you leave the stuff in the boxes
behind you, and it would have readied the petticoats,'
says she, 'I've had waiting for it these three months.'

'You're in a temper, little woman,' says he.

'And no wonder, when *she's* got three great boxes of it in
that house over there and I haven't a pinch I could throw
to the chickens,' says she.

'It's no matter what you have or haven't, for you're
clean beside yourself,' says her husband.

'O! ill luck to you, and ill luck is what you have and
anybody that's near you!' says she; 'and lop the ears off
me if the man who brought home those boxes doesn't get
the fruit of them; surely such fine boxes never had bad
stuff in them—each box lined all round inside with lead
as bright as a shilling.'

The husband was a fine, easy-going man, but, when she
put him in a passion, he went for the railer.

One day in the next week this woman visited the woman
who had dyed the petticoats again; and they were still

perfect. She had another story to tell about the stuff, and another use she was making of it—she had two ravenous pigs that were dying of hunger, and since she'd started boiling the stuff for them, mixed with a handful of meal, they lay at their ease, belly-upwards, in the yard. 'And pretty soon they'll be fine and fat,' says she.

'Wisha, ruin and decay on the man that never brought home a grain of it,' says the railing woman, 'and I have two famishing pigs ready to eat the children for hunger—all skin and bone though they're nearly a year old.'

'Yerra,' says the other woman, 'since the thing's done now, don't give it away that you mind.'

When this villain of a woman got home, she was spoiling for a fight, and grudged every minute till her husband came home. She dressed him up and down.

'Yerra,' says he, 'I'm not the only man, by a long chalk, that threw it away.'

'Devil a one except some fool like yourself,' says she.

She made him so savage in the end that the neighbours had to come and separate them.

Next morning the husband bestirred himself. He pretended that he was going to Dingle to get meal for the pigs. He borrowed bits of clothes from this man and that, and never stopped till he reached the town.

Some relations paid his fare, and he's never come back since.

The stuff in those boxes was tea—the first that ever came to the Island. We should know it well enough now.

9. *Gathering Seaweed*

ONE morning, I remember, I set my face to the shore. It was the season when we were getting seaweed for manure. I was bright and early, and had a fine, new fork with me for gathering any handful of weed that should come my way. When I came to the cliff above the strand, I leant with my breast against a little round-topped fence there, but there wasn't light enough to see anything from the top, and, that being so, I made my best speed down till I came to the pebbles. There was a little weed lying high and dry all along the line of the high tide, and I heaped it together with my fine new fork. I was by way of being rather set up with myself to think that I had done that much good work while the rest were asleep, but I fancy that kind of conceit never lasts a man long—and that's how it was with me, too.

After a bit I heard a hideous snore behind me, a queer sort of snoring that frightened me out of my wits, for there was nobody near me, and nobody coming towards me, and there wasn't much light in the morning yet. But I reflected that I should be a poor sort of chap, now that the day was coming, if I didn't go in the direction the snore was coming from, since I had a good weapon in my hand. No sooner was the word out of my mouth than I heard snore after snore. I swung round in a jiffy to where I heard them coming from, and what should I see but a huge great mottled seal, with his head in the air and the rest of his body stretched out on the sand. My heart leapt, though not for fear of the seal, for I knew that he could not do me any harm so long as I kept away from him and let him be. But the fear I had was that I shouldn't get him, for we thought more of one of them in those days than of the very finest pig. He stretched himself out to sleep again.

I saw now that it was a cow seal, and I plucked up courage, for I had always heard that it was an easier matter to kill seven of them than one of the bulls. She was lying at the edge of the water, and it was low tide. I looked to my fork while she was sleeping. I held the iron socket in my hand, with the handle stretched out in front of me, and started creeping up to her to fetch her a blow; but she lifted her head as though she had scented me, and gave vent to a loud, wild snort, and began to stir and to leave the nest she had made in the pebbles. As she turned towards the sea, I gave her a blow, six blows one after the other, but she paid no more attention to any of those blows with the haft than if it had been this pen in my hand that had struck her: and with one of them I broke the haft of the fork in two. I gave her a whack across the snout with the bit left in my hand, but she caught it in her mouth and chewed it, and made bits of it. All I had then was a stalk of the weed, and I showered blows on her with that as fast as I could, but I was doing her no harm, only that I was hindering her from getting to the water, which was not far from her by this time. In the end, when I was worn out, and she was, too, I managed to bang her on the top of the head with a lump of rock from the shore, and the blow turned her belly upwards, but she soon came to her senses again.

At last I thought she was dead, and I was still whacking away at her with a stalk of weed, when, what do you think? I went too close to her, and she had a shot at taking a bite out of me. And she managed it, too! She bit a huge lump out of my calf. As much as her four front teeth could get a grip of—all that she tore out of my leg. I didn't give in, though blood was flowing out of it in torrents, just as it was out of the seal.

Well, I'd finished the seal at last, and the seal had pretty nearly finished me, too, and it was like to be my last day when I looked closely at my leg and saw the lump out of it and the fountain of blood spurting. The last drop had nearly left my heart; I had to strip off my little vest and twist it round my leg, binding it with the cord from my waist. The water was coming up with the rising tide and the seal was not far from the edge, so that I was terrified that the sea would carry her off again from me after all my trouble; there was not a soul coming next or nigh me. It was the middle of the morning by now, and, as I thought the thing over, I cast a glance now and again at my leg, which was spouting a stream of blood.

At last, when my strength was nearly gone, I saw a man on the crest of the cliff, and he came down to me at full speed. It was an uncle of mine that we used to call Mad Diarmid. He was astounded, and said that he had never seen a seal of that size dead before.

'I've got the seal, uncle,' I said, 'but I've lost my leg.'

He staggered and nearly fell when he saw the great bite out of the leg. One man after another came down to us soon after that, and we carried the seal out of reach of the high tide and came home. My mother and father were in a terrible state when they saw the great hole in my leg, and they got little satisfaction out of the seal since the boy who had killed it hadn't got off with a whole leg. A crowd of them went off to skin the seal, with Mad Diarmid to direct them. My father didn't go at all. He was beside himself on account of my leg, but he sent the ass with Diarmid to bring it home, and he told him to give a slice of it to each man who helped in the skinning.

Old women were running in and out inquiring after my leg, every one with her own remedy. The old woman opposite came, too, quickly enough, and when she saw my leg: 'Yerra,' says she, 'there's not a pin's worth wrong with the leg.'

When she said that, I give you my word I was very grateful to her, for I thought it a better saying than the talk of the rest of them, which was that I should lose the leg. She said she had seen a bigger bite than that taken out of a man's leg by a seal in Inishvickillaun, and it didn't take a week for it to heal. Shaun Maurice Liam killed the seal that had taken the lump out of his leg. His father killed another seal, took a fresh piece of its flesh and placed it on the wound, then he bound it with a strip of cloth, and left it so for seven days. When he untied it, the hole had filled up with the natural flesh, so said the old hag.

'And how long after that was it before the skin grew on it?' said my mother.

'The very day the strip was taken off he went for a walk on the Island, without any covering on his leg, which was left bare to the sun, and that same evening the skin had grown on it,' says she.

My mother looked out and saw Bald Tom coming with a big lump of the seal on his back. One end of the lump touched the nape of his neck and the other end was down to his knee joint.

'Here comes Tom, Eileen,' says my mother to the hag.

She sprang up at a bound and ran out, and when she saw the fine burden her man was bringing her, she screamed with laughter. For a good while before that she had had nothing but a grain of rough salt to eat with her potatoes.

Then Diarmid came to the door with his ass, and nobody had ever seen an ass so heavily laden before. All you could see was his ears and his tail. All the rest was hidden with heavy lumps of seal, and the driver himself was bent down to the ground under his own load.

There was a loud burst of talking then, and, in the midst of all the chatter, my mother said:

'This lad will lose a leg by that seal, I'm afraid.'

'That he won't, believe me,' says Diarmid, 'since he managed to kill the seal; if he hadn't done that, he wouldn't have had much chance.'

Then mother told him what old Eileen had said.

'That certainly did happen, 'pon my soul,' says he. 'A bit from another seal was put in the hole from which the lump had been taken. And, my soul from the devil! by this time to-morrow you shall have a lump from another seal for your shinbone, my lad,' says Wild Diarmid.

The *Black Boar* left the Blasket harbour on the morrow morning, with a crew of eight, four oars, two sails, two masts, and two yards. There was a strong gale blowing hard from the north-east. She was a fine, big, new boat, and the crew knew their business. The sails were hoisted and they let her go with the wind. One of the men followed her along the hill with his pipe lit, and the boat was in Inishvickillaun before the pipe was cold in his mouth.

The man who lived in the island thought that she was a boat from a wreck or that half her crew were dead, and he was waiting for them up to his waist in the water of the creek, for there was a heavy swell running. He asked them at once what had brought them on a day like that.

'This is what brought us,' said Diarmid, telling his tale, 'and we won't leave the island without something alive or dead.'

' 'Pon my soul,' says the man of the island, 'you'll have your work cut out beyond anything you ever knew.'

The day was beginning to blow hard, and I was in and out of the house, for my leg wasn't sore or painful. Mother was up and down, too, listening to the loud wind like a hen with an egg, and after a bit she said:

'I'm afraid the men at sea will have to pay dear for their day's work to save your leg.'

However much I was afraid for my leg, and at the thought that maybe I should have to have a wooden leg, I was more worried about the *Black Boar* and all her crew at that moment.

The islandman took the men to his house and gave them something to eat. When they had eaten, he called for some of them to go with him to look for the seal. After they had searched every cave in the island, they failed to find a single seal. So they had to turn back home.

Diarmid went on terribly then, thinking that the boy with the leg must die. The islandman said there was still just one hole left, and that they would have to have twenty fathoms of rope to go into it—'and,' says he, 'I have a rope here that I use for getting sheep out of bad places.'

'Where's the rope?' says Diarmid.

He flung the rope over his shoulder and off he went, and the others with him. They lowered him down on the rope with a stick under his oxter to kill the seal, and a knife in his mouth. They paid out the rope till he was in the mouth of the cave, and then lowered the islandman after him.

That was a fine action of theirs, and I was grateful to them till the day they died. May their souls inherit the Kingdom of the Saints!

They brought the seal up with them, and, when they had him, the men said that no open boat could get home in such a storm. Diarmid said if they would set the sails for him, that she'd have to get back as she had come! Out they drove, into the great sea, and Diarmid fetched Slea Head on the first tack and the Blasket landing-place on the second, and he never stopped till he'd stuck a lump of the seal's flesh tight into my leg, and, a week after, I was as well as ever I was.

10. *Time Passes*

ONE Sunday a boat came in from Dunquin with a lady in it. Nobody recognized her till she was in their very midst. Who should it be but the daughter of the woman over the way. They kept on shaking hands with her till you would have thought her arm would have been wrung from her shoulder. She wore a picture hat, with a rakish feather or so sticking up from it. A yellow chain of glittering gold lay on her blouse. She carried a sunshade, and there was a twang in her speech, no matter which brogue she was talking—Irish or English. A box or two of all sorts came with her, and, best of all, she had a purse of gold from the States, for she was a master hand at putting it together.

It was impossible to know the good mare's foal, of course, for, though she was dressed up to the nines, there wasn't much more than the skeleton inside. She was never much of a figure, and, after she had spent five years in the land of sweat, she was uglier than ever.

A crowd followed her to their shanty. She had a bottle of whisky with her, and, as it was mostly the old women that went with her, it wasn't long till they were singing the old songs of Munster and praising the girl who had come back with something for them. They spent the day without a bite of food, for there was a taste of the drink for every singer for every song she sang.

It went on like this till Shrove came, and not much of it was gone before the Yank's money was being hawked about. As the old woman had been matching her with me

THE LOWER VILLAGE, THE WHITE STRAND,
AND THE ROCKS OF THE ROAD

HOUSES OF THE LOWER VILLAGE WITH BEGINISH BEYOND

when we were little ones, I took it into my head that maybe she'd start the same talk again, and no wonder as things were now. It would have been strange if it hadn't been so, for she was a girl with gold, and girls of that kind were few and far between in those days.

Before long, the grey woman, her mother, began to hint to my mother about all the gold Mary had and how she wanted to settle out on the mainland in some piece of land. 'Her father and I would rather she stayed near us,' says she. 'And if you like the idea, nobody's keeping her from you,' says she again.

'Yerra, this is how things are,' my mother said to her. 'Our boy's young yet, and I fancy it's not much use talking about anything of that kind to him. I don't think that he's very anxious to stay here, for maybe only himself and his sister would be left here of all the clutch, and, if it hadn't been to please us, I fancy he'd have gone before this.'

' 'Pon my soul, then,' says she, 'he's wrong there. Maybe he'd be in America a long time before he met a girl as good as she is.'

Early in Shrovetide Bald Tom went off to the mainland and found out a man and a bit of land that wasn't much good—the grass of a cow or two in a poor shelterless place that wouldn't encourage anybody. He gave very little fortune for it, for he was asked only for a little.

When he had everything ship-shape, Tom turned home and sent an invitation to the wedding to every house in the village. The grey woman didn't forget the house across the way, and I went to the wedding, like the rest. There was high feasting at every wedding in those days, all sorts of food and 'kitchen' and a swarm of people to eat it. There were eight barrels of porter there, and there wasn't a drop left in the bottom of one of them by morning.

When it was all over, everybody started for home. When we reached the cliff above the harbour at Dunquin, the

gulls themselves couldn't have left it: the swell was going
up over the green grass in every creek and cranny, and we
had to stay on the mainland that day and the next day
and the day after that again. We spent twenty-one days
altogether on land, if you please, and the day we went in
wasn't too good. I fancy none of them blessed the wedding,
they were so sore about it. She lived there for some time,
and had four children before she died.

When we got home the Island was full of wreckage. The
White Strand was covered with beams of red and white
deal, white planks, a fragment of a wrecked ship, a chair,
a stool, apples, and all sorts. The boat in which my father
worked got twelve baulks. Some of the others had more,
some less. The boat I was coming from the mainland in
came across a fine baulk in the middle of the Sound. We
had to use the sail rope to tow it, for we had no other rope
in the boat. After landing it, we set our faces to the sea
again. We came unexpectedly on two baulks next door to
one another. One of them was eighty feet long, and thick
to match. People said that it was the finest baulk that had
ever come ashore within living memory. We had no food
except a miserable potato or so in Dunquin that morning,
until the dark of night came, and by that time we had
saved eight baulks. But that was an unprofitable toil:
thirty shillings was all we got for the big fellow—in the
Great War that baulk would have fetched twenty pounds!

A dancing-master came on a visit to us for a time, and
he set up a dancing school for a month. Four shillings
apiece was his fee. The place he settled in was the old
monastery of the Soupers, that half of it in which the
school used to be in the old days. It had a plank floor which
made a great racket. The noise was the best part of the
proceedings—at first, anyhow. Not many put their names
down the first day, for few were in a position to pay.
Before long, however, they were coming to the school in

ones and twos. The teacher was a very good man, and had no fancy for turning out blunderers at a wedding feast. He had pocketed my four shillings, and I certainly got its value pretty soon as far as dancing goes, for the house where he lodged was near ours, and he used to give me a lesson whenever I ran across him. Before long I was a marvellous dancer—but, as always happens even to-day, somebody came to stop him from teaching anyone else, and the dancing school on the Island was put down.

A gentleman came on a visit to the Island soon after the break-up of the dancing school and he started all sorts of merry-making. Barret was his name. He had food and drink of every kind, cold, hot, and boiled. He brought eight bottles of whisky with him, and a variety of other drinks as well. It was a question who should sing him the first song, for they were shy till they saw that he had a good bottle of whisky to give to the first singer. They needed no pressure then, even those who hadn't sung a song for seven years or couldn't sing at all! It was the same story with the dancing; and the lilters got their glass, too!

The old women and the aged men danced also. I was half-tipsy most of the time, for the old women and the young girls would keep leading me out, as I was a fine dancer in those days. My father could dance, and he had been teaching me before the dancing-master came. The old women in particular took me out on the floor with them, and so I came home, half-seas over, every night all that week. If any of them had any rest, I hadn't, for I was dancing and singing and lilting turn and turn about: I was a clever fellow in those days!

Two boats from Iveragh were fishing lobsters that year. They were living in a shanty in Beginish with an Englishman in their company. Though the poor fellows used to be tired after the day's work they would find their way to the schoolhouse every night, and one of them was the best dancer that ever stood on a floor. He got plenty of glasses. They had a lilter, too, and you'd prefer him to any instrument of music.

The drink didn't last the whole week, as he had thought it would. He sent out a boat's crew to the nearest place, and fetched as much again. He must have remembered that week as long as he lived, and so did everybody else who had a share in the sport.

He sent a lot of presents to the Blasket after going home, and a pound of tobacco to the poet Dunlevy. The poet didn't let him go unthanked, for he wrote a poem in praise of him afterwards.

The next Shrovetide after this gentleman, Barret, had left the Island, a marriage proposal came to the King from Dunquin. He hadn't the style of *King* at that time, but, all the same, they were pretty well off. Probably he had plenty of other proposals, for he was a fine man in those days.

There was high feasting at the marriage, you may believe, for there were plenty there to make away with both food and drink. When they were going home, a boat turned bottom upwards in the Blasket creek. Two of the crew were underneath her. When they got them free, they were at their last gasp. Nursing mothers were milking their breasts and giving them the milk in a spoon. But after about an hour they took a turn for the better.

There were four other marriages in Dunquin the night of the wedding in the King's house, and the people of the parish came near to destroying one another. Little wonder, when you consider how much drink there was and all the scandal which had been talked for years before which now had a chance of venting itself. After the night's medley six of them had to be sent to hospital, and they didn't get off too lightly. One man had been hit with a bottle and another with a stone. One of them got a wipe with the tongs, like Owen Roe O'Sullivan when the woman hit him. Owen died, but this one pulled through.

When I was a young man the poet Dunlevy was composing his songs in the Island. The Island is a little place, you know, and we were always running up against one another every day in the year, in the houses or on the hill or at sea.

One day I wanted to go and cut some turf, for it was a very fine day, and we hadn't much of the old turf left to hand at that time. I went off through the door with a first-rate turf spade all ready and sharp. And though, as far as looks went, I was no match for the Fenians of old, nobody could say a word against me for what I was—I was quick and deft, and knew what was what.

Off I started up the hill, and my breath never came short, my foot had no cramp, my hand didn't shake, there was no pain in my heart till I came to a place where, thought I, there was good turf, and enough of it round me to do my business. I was wild to get to work and do my job. As I had no young folk in the house to bring me my dinner, only the two old people, I took a good hunk of bread with me in the morning—bread of coarse meal, very hard and yellow, only whitened outside with flour, like whitewash on a house wall; a pint bottle of milk from the cow, and a lump of butter about the size of a small potato. And, though no one has a word to say in favour of that sort of food nowadays, I was pleased enough with it then, for I had a mill in my mouth to grind it.

But I had little chance to turn my keenness for work to profit that day. I hadn't long begun on the job, working hard, when the poet Dunlevy came up with a spade under his oxter, to cut a bit of turf for himself; and there were a lot of others with him who had come out to the bog as he had, for it was a lovely day, and at that time there was very little of last year's turf that hadn't been burnt.

I fancy that no poet has ever been much good at carrying through any job that had any work in it except only poetry, and that was the way with Shane, too. I can produce some sort of evidence for this statement, for, whenever I take it in hand to compose quatrains (and I often do) I shouldn't be much use in a gang of workers or in the field so long as I was engaged upon them.

'Well,' says the poet, throwing himself down on a tussock, 'isn't it a pity for you to be cutting turf on such a hot day. Sit down a bit, the day is long and it'll be cool in the afternoon.'

I didn't care much for what he had to say, but I was rather shy of refusing to sit down with him. Besides, I knew that if the poet had anything against me, he would make a satire on me that would be very unpleasant, especially as I was just about coming out in the world. So I sat down beside him.

'Now,' says the poet, 'perhaps you haven't got the first poem ever I made. "The Black-faced Sheep", that was my first, and I had good reason for making it as far as provocation goes.'

Would you believe it—he started to recite every word of it, lying there stretched out on the flat of his back! There was a hummock of soft heather under him, and the scorching heat of the sun was flaming down from the cloudless, deep blue sky over our head, toasting the side of the poet that was uppermost.

I praised the poem to the skies, though it was vexing me sorely from another point of view—keeping me back from the profitable work that I had promised myself that morning should be done. The poet had put a stop to that with his babbling.

'The poem will be lost,' says he, 'if somebody doesn't pick it up. Have you anything in your pocket that you could write it down with?'

If a man isn't in luck's way in the morning and God's favour with him, the poor wretch can't hope to do much. The hapless Tom didn't cut as much turf as would make two loads for an old ass that day that he planned to do so much. And that was one of the first days that I felt the world going against me, for the fact is, for one day that went well with me, five would go wrong for me from that day out.

It wasn't to oblige the poet that I fished out my pencil and some paper I had in my pocket, but for fear he would turn the rough side of his tongue to me. I set about scribbling down the words as they came out of his mouth. It wasn't in the usual spelling that I wrote them, for I hadn't enough practice in it in those days.

I wasn't too happy then; and no wonder: a man who had a sensible bit of work on hand in the morning, and now it was laid aside for a pointless job! When once he'd opened his mouth, the poet had a jut on his jaw to send his voice out. I scribbled away at the words as best I could after a fashion that kept the poem more or less in my memory, and, besides, if a word should drop out here and there, the guide wasn't far from me, ready and willing to waste a bit of his life explaining it to me, even if the plough-team were waiting for him in the furrow.

When the pair of us had done with one another, the sun was sinking over the hill, and it was as much as Tom could do to keep his wits together by that time. When the poet had left me, the very first thing I did was to go to the tussock at the side of which my dinner was, and the dinner was utterly ruined: a horse couldn't have champed the hunk of yellow bread, and my milk had turned to stone in the bottle!

11. *My Manhood*

SINCE it had come about that the poet had put me back
that day I meant to do so much, so that I hadn't cut even
a load of turf, I fixed on another day for doing it. I didn't
take any dinner with me this day, for my mother told me
that she would send a little girl to me with a bit of hot food.

So it was. I ran up the hill and caught up with two
others who were in the same hurry as I was. On our way
to the mountain one of them glanced out to sea, and what
should he see but a school of fish down below us near in to
the rock.

'The devil!' says he. 'Look at all the fish shoaling!' Off
with us homewards as fast as we could. A boat was launched
and the nets were thrown into her: and we never stopped
till we had made the spot where the shoal was. It was still
on the surface, just as it had been. We made a cast of the
net and rowed round the shoal. We took as much as our
boat would carry, and there was enough for another boat
still in the net.

We had to land a man on the rock to fetch another boat
from the harbour to bring the catch home. They pitched
on me to go home and get the crew of the other boat, and
—though I say it myself—it wasn't easy to find my match
to get over the crest of the hill before me. When I reached
home, there weren't many men to be got, for they were all
at their own jobs.

There was only one boat with a seine net in the Blasket
that year. All the rest were little boats. It was one of those
that I had to get ready, and two old men were the crew that
came in it with me. Well, we managed it all right, for it

was a very fine day. When we reached the seine boat, we filled up the little boat with all she could take; but we were as badly off as before, for the net wasn't emptied yet. There was another boatful of fish still in it. We were in a dilemma, for there weren't enough men to make up the crew of another boat.

The shift we hit on was to send the little boat home with its load to land the fish and come back again. So it was done. She was given four oars and a man to steer her. And it wasn't long till she was back again. The net was heaped into her, and she was full to the chin. Off went the two boats together, both of them down to the gunwale. The fish was May mackerel, every one of them as long as your arm. The old men said that they had never seen a finer catch of fish in a single seine net.

The next thing was to cure the fish; a hard job it was washing it and salting it, for there was no market for fresh fish at that time. There were eight thousand fish in the great heap, for it was large-sized fish. We were pretty well worn out after the day's fishing, and we had a good night's sleep, never fear.

Early in the morning there was a knock at our door. My mother got a surprise, for she it was who opened the door. Who should be there but the old woman's son, collecting men to fetch the priest to his mother, who had been very bad since the middle of the night. My mother gave me a call—I was fast asleep at the moment. I sprang up. I had no wish to fail to do my share of the duty of helping to bring the priest to her. I dressed myself, and my mother got ready a saucepan of warm milk while I was dressing. I bolted it and a hunk of bread, and out of the door I went. I managed to be one of the first who got to the harbour, but they were coming up, man after man, till we were all collected. It was a fine, soft morning, only rather dark. Off we went and came to Dunquin. And the sick woman's son went to Ballyferriter parish to get the priest, with another lad in his company.

The day was passing, and there was not a sign of man or dog with news, but at last, as the day drew to its end, the priest came, but he had nothing to tell us of the other two, for they had made their call on him early in the day. We launched the boat, took the priest aboard, and made our best speed to sea, home to the Blasket. We weren't far out from the land when a heavy mist descended, so that you couldn't see to put your finger in your eye, but we kept on rowing for a good bit, though we caught no glimpse of land or any house. We were at work so long that we grew weary, and we realized that we were lost and that it was useless to keep on working, so we stopped for some time. Then the priest asked us if we had given up hope. We answered that we had, for we should have reached land long ago if we hadn't gone astray. The priest started on his breviary, and at that very moment one of the men looked out and saw a rock or crag, and off we started towards it, but, alas! we were three miles out of our way.

Well, it began to lift a bit and we managed to make the landing-place, and it was evening by this time. The priest didn't stay long, but came back to us immediately, and off we started again. It was late evening by the time we got out to the mainland again. One of our men looked, and what should he see but the two good-for-nothings down by the shore with blood streaming from them, for they had been rising and falling with the drink they had taken. I say nothing of one of them. But what of the man, the old woman's son, whose mother was at death's door? We returned home, and that day was no holiday for us, any more than was the day on which we had made the great catch of fish.

So does a man's life wear away, and a great deal of it to little profit. I had spent my week without getting any turf, as I had proposed at its beginning, though I had caught plenty of fish.

A day or two after that the grey woman died. And that meant more work: to go to the town and bring home what was needed for the wake. It is the custom for those who fetch the priest to go for the things for the wake. And so you may be sure I had a hand in all that was going on, for the son came to my threshold—and, of course, it wasn't a refusal I gave him. Off we went in the great seine boat, eight of us with four oars, two men apiece to three of the oars, one on the other oar and a man at the rudder. We got to Dunquin. He arranged for a horse, and they started off. There were three men in the cart, two from the Island, and the driver; and a woman with them. It is an ancient custom for a woman to go with those who get the things for a wake.

I stayed behind in Dunquin. Although I said nothing, I fancied the cart wouldn't be back very quickly. All the same it was. They had good stuff for the old hag's wake with them. You could get a pint of porter there, too, and a glass of whisky. She was taken ashore on a magnificent day, only her family burial place was a good way off, in Ventry churchyard. There was a tavern in that parish, and it was a regular custom for those who followed the funeral to have a drinking bout there. Most of us went in there that day, too. Anybody who didn't go in made his way home, and it was pretty late in the day before we got there. The rest stayed in Ventry parish till the next day, and came home about noon. That was the last end of the grey woman opposite, and I can tell you that, if it wasn't my luck to be rich the day she left the world, it wasn't for want of her good wishes. I hadn't a thing to say against her.

Well, so that was done with. But the dead don't feed the living, and every one of us began to think of what most needed doing. Since it was the turf-cutting season, we were all making for the hill, every man starting out as soon as his preparations were made. My own spade was in the bog every day, and nothing mattered, I thought, so long as I could have the turf cut before the dry season set in. The thought gave me no rest till I had my hand on the haft of the spade. I was working away splendidly for the most part of the day, and I had a good bit of work done when all the young girls of the Island came upon me, going out to drive the cows home. They set upon me, one of them pulling my ear, another snatching the spade out of my hands, two others looking for a chance to tip me over on the flat of my back in the bog to have some fun out of me. If one didn't think of a trick another had it in a second.

I knew perfectly well that I'd cut my last sod of turf that day when I saw the mop head of the first of them coming between me and the daylight. For the gang of girls we had in the Island in those days were next door to being half wild. And, though I was pretty tired before they came, sure it was they that finished me altogether. And no wonder—six girls, just about beginning to ripen, running over with high spirits, whatever sort of food and drink they had. It's easy baking when you have meal to hand, and so it was with them: stout, strong hoydens, as healthy as the fish in the sea; it made no odds to them what sort of food they had on the table, and they didn't care.

The worst they could do to me didn't vex or worry me, be sure of that. It would have been an odd thing, indeed, if it had, for it was the wild spirit of youth that was driving them, and sure I had a good right to have a spark of the same fire touching me up, too, for there was many a young man of my own kind who'd rather have them playing their games with him than all the turf on the hills.

One day soon after this—that is to say, the day I meant to finish with the turf till the next year (if I lived)—what should come my way but the very same gang of girls. They used to be driving the cows home and playing all sorts of mad tricks as they did so. Of course, they spied me out. They were on me at once, throwing things at me, and up to every mischief. Since I was putting the last hand to the turf-cutting, I promised myself that I would spend the rest of the evening having fun with them. There wasn't one of the six, if I had given her the wink, that wouldn't have gone with me ready and willing for the knot there's no untying; but, whoever I had my eye on in those days, it wasn't any one of those six. Never mind—it would do me no great harm to have a bit of fun with them, and I had it all right. If I felt any weariness, it left me then, for those six went for one another again and again, and no sooner were they up than they'd be down again, one overturning the other, and the same with me, too. It's long I remembered that afternoon; I remember it still. Says the poet: 'Bothering with women never did a man any good!' and that's just how it was with me, for they sent me astray from my work from that time out.

Well, as I said about these girls, that it looked as though I wasn't going to get on with my job for some time to come because of them, I was right: for, when I saw them heaped hugger-mugger on top of one another that afternoon, it came into my head that the best thing I could do was to get one of the kind for a wife for myself—and it was high time, too!

12. *The Day of the Seal Hunt*

I HAD the turf cut now, and was fairly satisfied, only there was a great deal of work to be done on it as soon as it dried: and the beginning of the dry season was making itself felt already. My plan was to spend another day in fixing up a good shelter, so that all I should have to do would be to throw the turf in when it was dry, for it would hold me up if I left it till later.

The day I decided on for this was a wild, gusty, dry day, just right for the job I had in hand, and off I went up the hill. When I got there, I stripped to the shirt, for the place where I was going to work was well sheltered.

I set to work right in the very midst of an old stone structure that had never been shifted for forty or sixty years before, and began to set it to rights, designing a new shelter. I had a pup with me, and I noticed nothing till he had slipped between my legs and ran back under an overhanging flagstone that projected far out, with a hollow space beneath it. My pup went so far into the hole under the stone that I couldn't see a trace of him.

Well, I'd lost my fine dog—and a fine dog he was, too. He had a reputable name, for we had gone as far back as the Fenians of old to fetch it for him. Oscar was what we called him. The pup had ruined my day's work for me and put an end at once to all my energy and determination. I started to bend down and peer under the hollow of the stone, and I managed to see about an inch of the tip of his tail. So I began to call him out, but that wasn't much good, and I realized that he was stuck there. I was in a queer fix then. My new shelter wasn't made yet; my pup was lost, and I was terrified of what my father would say, for he it was who had brought the pup from Dingle, carrying him for eight miles in a basket on his back. I had a big fishing hook in my pocket and a good bit of twine, so I tied it to the handle of the turf-spade and thrust it back into the hole as far as I could. The hook stuck into the top of the pup's behind. I dragged him towards me, and out he came easily enough, with a lump of a rabbit in his jaws; the rabbit was dead, and the pup had eaten one of his front paws, and, when I pulled it out of his mouth, he gave one leap back into the hole again. When I looked for him again, I couldn't see a sign of him. I was beside myself. I failed to get him out of the hole again, and late in the evening I had to go home in a very bad humour.

I got home in a pretty bad temper and hung up the rabbit. My meal was ready, of course, and I went up to the table.

'I expect,' said my mother, 'that it was the pup that caught the rabbit for you.'

'It was,' said I, 'and he's left himself for a forfeit.'

'How did he do that?' says she. 'Did he go over the cliff?'

I told her the whole story from beginning to end—how I fetched him out with the hook, and he dived into the hole again at once. 'And he'll stay there for good and all,' I told her.

'Don't mind if he does,' says she.

My father never breathed a word while this talk was going on, and I thought that he was saving it up for me, and that I should hear what he had to say soon enough: for I fancied that he would think that it was by my own carelessness I had lost the pup.

But often things turn out differently from what we expect. And so it was with me and my father, for when he did speak, there was good sense in what he had to say.

'I believe,' said he, 'that Oscar would never have gone back into the hole if he hadn't scented another rabbit there —possibly two, or even three of them.'

There's nothing children like to hear more than a friendly word from a good father and mother, and that was my case then, for, though I'd been upset enough when I came down from the hill, the worst thing for me had been what I expected to hear from them. As it was, they dispersed all my fear; and things remained like that until the morrow.

If ever I slept late, it wasn't that next morning, as my head was full of thoughts of the pup. So I was up at break of day. I took a bite or two and drank a cup or so of milk. My mother heard me, and asked where I was off to so early: 'Surely you have the whole long day before you, and,' says she, 'do you see your father around?'

'No,' said I.

'He left his bed a while back, and I fancy he went up the hill.'

I had no difficulty in believing this, and, when I was ready, off I went after him. And once I'd started I never stopped until I had reached the spot where I had been at work. The first thing I saw coming towards me was Oscar. He ran up to me pretty soon, and you'd have thought that he hadn't seen me for half a year when he caught sight of me. My father was standing on the flagstone. He'd just got Oscar out, with five huge rabbits, pulled out of the hole along with the pup. My father was cleverer than I was, for he'd made a channel at the end of the stone, in the place where he guessed the end of the hole would be, and when he thrust his hand in, he found a rabbit, and then two, till he had five of the finest rabbits that were ever taken out of a single hole. He flung them across his shoulder and went off home. I finished my new turf shelter.

I had planned to have a rest when I had the turf cut and the shelter ready for throwing it in when it was dry; but I didn't get it, my lad! My father had always been a first-rate man in his youth and afterwards, and it was a constant saying of his that nobody ever got anything properly done who lay abed on the flat of his back when the sun was shining in the sky, and that it was bad for the health, too.

Well, whatever he was in the habit of saying, I had arranged with myself to have an extra bit of bed this morning before starting on another job. But before long I heard somebody talking loud. A man spoke by the hearth and asked was Tom awake yet. My mother said no.

'Why do you ask?' says she.

'There's a boat going after seals,' says he.

The speaker was an uncle of mine on my mother's side. At first I thought it was my father speaking, but no—he had gone back to the strand.

I leapt up and, when I'd had a bite, crammed some food into my pocket and set out for the boat. All the rest were ready before me, with everything necessary to get the best of the seals: ropes to drag them out of the cave when they should be dead, and a big, stout club with a thick end to it —we should want that right enough to lay them low. Off we went out of the creek.

Another boat had left early in the morning, but they had taken the direction of the Lesser Blaskets. They had fetched up at Inishvickillaun—a famous place for seals in the caves—for there are a lot of caves in that island.

You need calm weather and a good spring tide. Well, we put out the four oars, 'tough, sweet-sounding, enduring, white, broad bladed', as was the way with the boats of the Fenians of old so often, and stayed not from our headlong course till we reached the mouth of the cave we had fixed on.

The cave was in the western end of the Great Island. It was a very dangerous place, for there was always a strong swell round it, and it's a long swim into it, and you have to swim sidelong, for the cleft in the rock has only just room for a seal. When the boat stopped in the mouth of the cave there was a strong suck of swell running. Often and again the mouth of the hole would fill up completely, so that you'd despair of ever seeing again anybody who happened to be inside, and that left those of us who were in the boat little to say. The only young men there were myself and another lad, for the likes of us were not experienced enough for the job. It needs grown men, well on in years.

The captain of the boat spoke and said: 'Well, what did we come here for? Isn't anybody ready to have a go at the hole?'

It was my uncle who gave him his answer: 'I'll go in,' said he, 'if another man will come with me.'

Another man in the boat answered him: 'I'll go in with you,' says he.

He was a man who stood in need of a bit of seal meat, for he spent most of his life on short commons. He had a big family, and none of them old enough to give him any help.

The two made their preparations. There was a bridge of rock across the mouth of the cave, with the water above and beneath it. Two men had to stand on the bridge to help the other two in. One of the two was a good swimmer, but not my uncle. The swimmer went in first, carrying the end of the rope in his mouth, the slaughtering stick under his oxter, a candle and matches in his cap and the cap on his head. It was useless to go into the cave without a light, for it penetrated too far under the ground. My uncle followed him, another rope tied round him, and his hand gripping the swimmer's rope, one end of which was tied up somewhere inside, while its other was fastened to the bridge outside so as to be always ready.

The other youngster and I stayed on the bridge to drag out the seals from the two inside. They kindled a light, and when they reached the end of the cave, there was a beach full of seals there—big and little, male and female. *Bainirseach* is the name of the female seal, and the male is called the bull. There are some of them that it's absolutely impossible to kill.

The two inside made themselves ready for the great enterprise before them. Each of them had a club, and they aimed a blow at every one of the seals. They had a lighted candle on a boulder. Both of them had a flannel shirt on, dripping, of course, from the salt water it had come through. When they had finished the slaughter and all the seals there were killed, they had more trouble in front of them. Many of the seals were very heavy, and the cave was a most awkward place: there were great boulders between them and the water, and the passage out was a very long one. But there's no limit to the strength a man has when he's in a tight place, and those two, handling the dead bodies of the seals there on the beach underground, worked like horses. They dragged every one of eight seals down to the water, and by the time they had done, the swell burst into the cave, and the two of us who were on the bridge had to grip the rock wall high up.

When that stress was past, there came a calm, and one of the men inside shouted to us to drag the rope out. We thought that one of themselves was on the rope, but it wasn't so. Four huge seals were tied to it. We had to pass the end of the rope to the boat, and, when the seals had been lifted in, to send it into the cave again. This rope was fastened to the rope that remained stretched into the cave, and the man who was with me on the bridge shouted out loud to them to draw it in again, and they did so in double quick time. Before long those inside called to us to drag it back again. The swell was raging mad by this. When we drew in the rope, there were four other seals tied to it, though we expected that it would be one of the men themselves. We had to do as we had done before and send the rope in again. Every now and then we were forced to leave the bridge from the great seas that swept over it, filling up the mouth of the cave too.

It was the swimmer who took to the rope first to make his way out, leaving it to the other man to use the fixed rope. It took the swimmer in the passage a long time to reach the bridge, there was so heavy a swell. He got there in the end, with his flannel shirt torn to tatters. My uncle— who, as I said before, couldn't swim a stroke—started on the last rope. The rise and fall and suck of the swell made it hard for us to pull him to the bridge. In the middle of it all, the rope broke, and the wave swept him back with it into the cave again. My heart was in my mouth when I saw him going down. I thought he was lost. I plunged down from the bridge into the submerged cave. My foot struck the end of the broken rope under water. By God's grace I brought off my good uncle safe and sound, but we had a desperate struggle for it. I was a good swimmer in those days.

Our big boat was loaded down to the gunwale with four cow seals, two bulls, and two two-year-olds—one for each of the crew. Every one of the men had a barrelful of seal meat, and we reckoned in those days that every barrel of seal meat was worth a barrel of pork. The skins fetched eight pounds.

It's odd the way the world changes. Nobody would put a bit of seal meat in his mouth to-day. They melt it down for light, for it is cram-full of oil. Moreover, if you made a present of the skin to a gentleman, he'd hardly deign to accept it from you. It's long since anybody tried to do anything with one of them but throw it to the dogs. Yet in those days they were a great resource for the people, both the skin and the meat, and you could get a pack of meal for one of them. And anywhere you liked to take a lump of seal's flesh you could get the same weight of pork for it, if there were any in the house. People don't know what is best for them to eat, for the men that ate that kind of food were twice as good as the men of to-day. The poor people of the countryside were accustomed to say that they fancied they would live as long as the eagle if they but had the food of the Dingle people. But the fact is that the eaters of good meat are in the grave this long time, while those who lived on starvation diet are still alive and kicking.

13. *A Wife proposed for Me*

THE year 1878 (or about that) was a fine year for potatoes and fish and turf, and it was no hard task for poor folk to pass the time on a bit when things went well with them like that. Usually in a year of this kind there was much talk of marriages. Round Christmas time this year there was a fat sheep hanging up in every house in the Island and rabbits were plentiful, and meat from the town.

I fancy there was no village in the countryside in which meat was so common as it was in the Island at that time. There'd be a bottle of whisky or so, too, either given or bought. I remember the time when there was only one pot-oven in the Island, and it never left the fire for the seven days of the week.

In those days one of the Dalys lived in Inishvickillaun as a herd, and he had a great time of it in the island—that is, when his children were grown up. There was a great demand for the kind of fish known as lobsters, and the herd's children were grown men at the time and had a boat of their own. In those days I myself spent night after night there, for we used to be fishing in the far island all the time, and if we hadn't any fish to take home, we used to run the boat ashore; for that was what the old couple in the house had told us to do.

The people used to say that they were the best couple that had ever stood on the rock. They had five sons and five daughters, the finest family of children, take them for all in all, that any couple had had for many a long day. I was the only young man in the boat, and, that being so, the young folk and I had a deal to say to one another, and, before long, one of the daughters and I were making up to one another. She was a very fine girl, and the best singer going in her day. We'd made many a call there that season, and had a very good time. The year remained fine for us up to Christmas.

The man on the rock had two splendid pigs, and, as they had always been so good to us, we promised them that we would go to fetch the pigs next week. One fine day in that week my uncle ran in one morning—the uncle for whom I had run into such danger in the seal cave the day the rope broke.

'What's your hurry to-day?' said I.

'Hurry enough, my lad! We shall have a fine day to-day, and we'll go to get the pigs, and maybe if anybody's slow to go there, it won't be you!'

'Yerra, why so?' says my mother.

'Ye, God help you, if that's the way with you!' says he. 'Aren't all the young women on the rock running wild after him—and they're a handsome lot there! You ought to be wanting the help of one of them hard enough by rights.'

'Be up in two leaps,' said he to me then.

We went to the rock. When we were starting out from the house with the pigs to the harbour, the old woman of the house handed her husband a bottle of whisky to serve round to us. No woman in her day had a better name for kindness than she had, though I should be sorry to say a word more in praise of her than of her husband, so far as my acquaintance with them went.

We never gave the pigs rest till we'd placed them in the boat—two fine pigs, a year old. The woman herself and one of her daughters—the girl my uncle Diarmid was always matching with me—went with us. Out we put to sea. Up went the sails. We had a fair wind with us all the way to the creek in the Great Blasket. We landed them there that day so that they might go out with the Island pigs on the morrow.

Next day, when we had eaten, everybody who had a pig or two pigs was making ready to start for the land. I had a fine pig of my own, and my uncle Diarmid had one nearly as good. They were both of them put into the boat, with another belonging to one of the villagers, the two pigs from the Inish, the woman from the Inish, and her daughter. It was a big boat, and the number I have reckoned up filled it pretty well. They were set on shore in Dunquin, and the boat went home again. There were a boat or two, besides, out with pigs, and they went home, too. Off we started along the road, walking, with our pigs. About half-way Diarmid's pig struck; the road was hurting her; she was a very heavy animal, with poor feet. But Diarmid had a friend by him this time.

'Stay by the pig,' says he to me, 'and my soul from the devil but I'll fetch something quickly that'll lift her off the soil of Ireland.'

I had to do what he asked me, though my own pig could have walked to Tralee. The women from the Inish and I and the pigs waited together until Diarmid came back with a good horse and a creel on the cart. The driver was an uncle of Diarmid's, and of my mother, too.

We threw Diarmid's pig in, and that was the stiffest job of work I'd ever known in my life up to then—the driver and my uncle joined hands under the forepart of her, while I had to lift her rear, and the weight would have been altogether too much for me if the Inish woman hadn't lent me a hand. We looked over the other pigs then to see which of them showed most signs of being tired, and we lifted mine and one of the Inish pigs into the cart.

There wasn't room for the fourth one, and we started off. When we found that it held us up too much to wait for the walking pig, the driver and my uncle went off with the others, and were to come back again to pick up the fourth. We continued to walk along, and we had got as far as the corner of the pier in Dingle before they came to us. It wasn't worth while to lift him into the cart then, so we drove him along on his feet. At the corner of the quay Diarmid gave him a slash with a switch he had in his hand. That hurt him, so he swerved, and off he went, helter-skelter, down the quay. The driver got in front of him, but he ran between his legs and carried him off and flung him on the flat of his back out in the sea, and went with him himself.

Diarmid got a hold of the driver, who was only just in the water, and pulled him up, very sorry for himself. The pig faced out to sea.

'Holy Mary! the poor woman's pig is drowned,' says Diarmid to me. 'And isn't it a shame, and she such a decent woman!'

I could see that he was getting at me to save the pig, though he didn't like to tell me straight out to go swimming after it. There wasn't a boat or an oar in the harbour that wasn't in use, and I should have been sorry to see the pig go down. I snatched the switch from my uncle's hand and ran down the quay. I threw off my clothes and plunged in from the end of the quay. Diarmid spoke from above:

'Whatever you do, don't get tangled up with the pig or he'll drown you,' says he.

He needn't have told me that; but he was terribly afraid for me.

I came up with him pretty quickly and turned him in to land. I had to take the switch out of my mouth and make use of it before I could face him for the land. When he reached the slip, the driver got him by the ear: it was

easy enough to hold him now, however it had been when
he floored him in his flight. I swam back to my clothes.
The pigs were driven into a house. The driver had a drink
or two, and then went off home.

'Come along, uncle,' said I, 'and we'll have a bite of
food.'

We went into a house where there was food to be had,
and both made a thoroughly good meal. Then we went
to look up our friend to whose house every Islander who
came to Dingle always made his way. He began bargaining
for our pigs. He had already looked them over. Diarmid
and he managed to come to terms quickly, and then they
came to me. He gave five pounds ten for Diarmid's pig,
and before long he had my pig, too, for six pounds. We'd
only just finished our business when the two women from
the Inish came in through the door. I turned to the host
and told him to give them any drink they fancied, but the
old woman said at once that they ought rather to stand
me one, for they'd have lost their pig if it hadn't been
for me.

'For Mary's sake,' said Diarmid, 'let him be. It won't do
him much damage to stand us a drink when he's just got
six pounds clear for his pig.'

'Who bought them?'

'The man of this house bought both his and mine,' says
Diarmid.

What I did was to give Diarmid half a pint.

'Look here,' says I, 'take that into that room. I'll come
to you later.'

'But where are you going?' says Diarmid.

'O, a small job; I won't be two minutes.'

'O, by Mary! we'll have no fun at all if that's the way.'

I had a good reason for going. I wanted some braces,
for my breeches only depended on a bit of string from back
to front. My old braces were all in tatters with the work

I'd had with the pigs since the first day we went to the Inish until now.

I left them there and went off to a clothes shop.

'Yerra, welcome from the West,' says the woman in the shop.

'May you live to be a hundred, good woman,' was my answer to that. It wasn't for her deserts that I called her 'good woman'—for I had reason often enough to know that there wasn't much to be said in her praise—but by way of good manners.

She was asking me questions about this and that, and glancing at me now and again all the time to see when I'd begin to ask for what had brought me. Every now and then I'd put a hand in my pocket, and her eyes danced in her head, one on the shop and the other on me.

'Show me a pair of braces,' I said at last. I'd have left her to suffer a while longer without showing her my money if it hadn't been that I was losing all the fun of Diarmid and his half-pint, for I knew he'd give me sport—that's why I'd left it in his hand when I came away. The shop-woman got out a pair of braces at once.

'These are a shilling a pair,' says she. 'They're imported braces.'

I took a pair of them in my hand, and saw at once they were no good.

'Give me the very best, if you have them,' said I. 'If those are imported goods, keep them till customers are imported to buy them from you.'

I scored calmly off the shopwoman, and another woman who was there burst out laughing. The shop-woman flushed up. Then she brought out the old kind. I chose a pair of them, handed her a shilling, and out I came.

When I came back to Sunshine Diarmid—and well he earned the name by this time—every soul in Goat Street was collected round him. Some of them were sitting on stools, some standing up. The house was full, for all the Islanders who had come with pigs had turned up by now, and the drink was circulating fast. The old woman from the Inish was singing 'For Ireland I won't tell her name', and you'd leave food untouched to listen to her. And her daughter was better than she was.

A man spoke to me and said: 'The fairy music is a-singing.'

We went on like that far into the night—the women singing and the men drinking, all of them talking louder and louder and their wits gone wandering.

All of them took lodgings in the town that night. On the morrow morn there were plenty of pigs and people about. That was a day of drink and good company in Dingle. Each lot of us picked out his own bar. Every family had relations there, and preferred to spend their money in their kinsman's house. We went to the house of the man who bought our pigs from us and sat there. The two from the Inish were with us. Others from the country-side gathered round us—some of them relations of ours and others who had no connexion with us.

A lot of them spied out Diarmid the Joker. They knew well enough that they would have fun with him, and sure enough they had. Round went the drink. The old woman from the Inish stood the first drink, half a gallon of porter, for the boat's crew that had brought in the pigs were there.

Jolly Diarmid shook her hand, and came over to me and shook my hand, too.

'Tune up a song to raise my heart after the week's work,' says he.

I knew better than to refuse him, for he'd make a laughing-stock of me. 'The Dark Woman's Smooth Hill', that was my song, and few spoke till I had finished it. If there were two better than me, there were three worse.

The old woman sang the second song, and she was splendid at it. 'The Soft Deal Plank' was the song the girl, her daughter, sang, and she sang it faultlessly. The drink was being drunk and drawn like anything till everyone had his fair share taken. The house and the pavement outside it were crowded.

Before long I saw a big fellow pushing his way through the people, and he spoke: 'By your leave, men,' says he, and he never stopped till he got to me, and he wrung my hand seven times over. 'Devil carry me! I'd have cleared off home before long and never heard you singing a song!' says he, banging on the table. 'Half a pint of whisky here!' says he. 'Yerra, wisha! out with your voice, if you please,' says he.

We knew one another well, for often before that I'd had to sing him a song. He was a great drinker, but he was decent in his drink. The half-pint came at once, and I couldn't refuse. I had to toss off a glass. Then the music started. Well I remember the song I sang that day. 'For Ireland I won't tell her name', that was it, for I knew well that was the one the big man liked best, for often before had I sung it for him. When it was finished, the big man sent round drinks again.

'I wonder,' says he to me, 'if there's anybody else here to sing a song?'

'There is, my boy,' said I, pointing out the two women from the Inish.

They didn't refuse him, and what did they do but start together, the two of them, to sing the song, for they were mother and daughter. It was no great marvel, for one of them was born of the other. I'm sure that most of that company felt as I felt, that I would cheerfully have spent two days and two nights without food or drink listening to the singing of those two.

When the song was ended, the big man **shook hands**

with them both heartily, and he did the same to me, as it was I who had guided him to that fairy music: and he beat upon the table again and called for another half-pint. A shilling was the price of a half-pint in those days. It costs nine shillings this very day of writing. He put the bottle in my hand to share it out. One would take it from me for two who didn't. I saw Sunshine Diarmid in the corner piping noisily away, for he had drunk his fair share, and I said to myself that I should have to spend another night in the town.

Before long the big man turned to me again and shook me by the hand.

'I should like to hear another of your songs before we start for home,' says he. 'It'll be a good while, maybe, before we run across one another again.'

I gave in to him, of course. I sang a song or two, and the women from the Inish sang three of them, and another on the top of that, and, when it seemed to me that it was getting on for the time for going home, the company didn't agree with me. At last, late in the day, at the time of the wool market—that's always the latest of all the markets—the time to be making our best speed on the homeward road, Diarmid was getting wilder and wilder, and never thinking of his little home, nor would he have given it a thought before Christmas so long as the drink was going its rounds.

I spoke crossly to him, and said that surely it was high time for us to be getting along home, now we had two days and two nights away. But he only rushed up to me and started mauling me with kisses.

I spoke to the woman from the Inish and gave her the same hint.

'Yerra, wisha,' says she, 'this is a day of our life, and we shan't always be in the way of a day like it.'

I should know how to deal with answers of that kind

to-day, perhaps, when I am old, but in those days I was young and light-headed. I had to bring my uncle back home—and he'd left a houseful of children behind him, some of them with pretty empty bellies until the money for the pigs should bring them something. As for the woman from the Inish, she had only left two stones of yellow meal in that island of the sea, and yet neither she nor Diarmid let the thought of house or home worry them the least bit. When I had thought of all this, I gave up altogether and said to myself that I was done with giving them advice, but would agree with whatever they said; and so it was.

A lot of them had cleared out of the public-house by this, but the big man was still there. The woman from the Inish was talking to him, and in the course of the conversation she said she'd have to hire a horse from the town to Dunquin next day.

'If I'd been keeping my eye on the carts from the countryside since morning, my things would have been there to-night,' says she.

'Have you got a load?' said he to me.

'I shall have about half a sack of meal,' said I.

'Diarmid will have something, too,' says he.

'Certainly he will,' said I. Diarmid hadn't a ray of sense left by this time.

'I pledge my solemn word that I shall be here by eight o'clock to-morrow morning, if I live,' says he.

He put to his horse and drove off down the main street, and I daresay he wasn't long getting home.

I turned in again to the rake, Diarmid. He could hardly stand.

The woman from the Inish came in after me.

'Come along,' said I to him, 'we'll be getting home, or haven't you any feeling for the lump of a wife you've left behind you?'

'Well, she's no beauty,' says he. 'She'll be all right.'

We dragged him out with us, and made our way to a house where we would get some food. They put good food before us, but we ate very little of it. I went off to bed, and fell asleep very soon. It was far on in the night when my uncle came. He fell asleep at once, and slept like the dead. I had another nap, and when I came to myself again morning was breaking and day was coming. I stayed awake, for I said to myself that the man with the cart would be along soon—that is, if he was a man of his word. I never dreamed that he would be there as early as he proposed, but I hoped that he'd come along some time that day, for he was a sensible sort of fellow.

I hadn't been turning over these thoughts for long when I heard the rattle of a cart, but it never passed through my head that it was the big man so early as that. Yet I was wrong, for it was he all right. He put up his horse in his usual place and came to us. We waited till breakfast was ready, and then started to collect our things into the cart, for we'd packed them up the day before. Diarmid the mad was not yet himself, nor near it. However, off we went helter-skelter out of the town, after spending three days and nights there.

We faced for Dunquin and got there fast enough. A boat had come out to fetch the woman of the Inish. The man with the cart bade us farewell and turned towards Bally-ferriter, his own place.

We went down to the boat at once and set sail for the Great Blasket. We didn't shift the provisions for the Inish out of the boat, for Diarmid had planned to go back with them, take some hunting tackle with us, and bring a fine load of rabbits with us on our return.

I couldn't escape, though I wasn't very keen to go there after Dingle; but Diarmid was my mother's brother, and, besides that, there was the girl. She and I were always making up to one another. So we hoisted the sails again,

THE HARBOUR

TRANSPORTING A COW TO THE MAINLAND

and off we went at full speed till we reached Inishvickil-laun. We spent two days and nights in that rock, bringing lots of rabbits back with us every evening, singing song after song every night till one o'clock, and sleeping till high noon. My uncle never stopped trying to make a match between me and the girl, every night and all the time, and no doubt there was a touch of cunning at the back of this, for she took good care that the two of us had our share of any good things that were going all that time, whether her people knew it or not.

On the morning of the third day it wasn't too fine and we made our preparations for starting home. We were all loaded down as we went to the boat, and every soul in the island followed us to the water. They were thoroughly down in the mouth because we were going. I may as well admit that, whatever was the case with the others, I wasn't too cheerful, and no wonder, for I was leaving behind me the merriest days I had ever known, and, into the bargain, I was turning my back on the girl I liked best in the whole blessed world right then.

Well, we shifted off home, and the people there were pretty jealous of us. We had a cargo of fat rabbits, and all those who had stayed behind had was seaweed and turf and manure.

14. *Christmas Provisions*

WHEN we got home, Bald Tom was at his last gasp, in need of a priest. At the end of the night there was a knock on our door, and my mother called me and said that Paddy was waiting for me to go with him to fetch the priest for his father, who was breathing his last.

I couldn't fail him now, since I'd fetched the priest for his mother. Besides, I realized that there are some people that no ill wind goes by without putting them to some trouble or other. There were some of closer kin to Tom than I who were left to have their sleep out that day.

I had a bit to eat and off I went out of the door. Paddy wasn't long in bringing the priest to Dunquin, and the whole trip was over very soon. Tom was dead the next day. Then there was another journey for the wake and another for the burying. That's how I spent my month from the first day we fetched the pigs from the Inish till the day we laid Bald Tom in the churchyard in Ventry.

Paddy was planning to move to another little house higher up; and so he did. It was a wreck of a place just opposite the house we had then. He was married by this.

It was now the beginning of the Christmas month. All fishing was at an end, and the Islanders set about manuring their ground. Late and early we were at it, raking away; and that was our practice in the Island every year up to St. Bridget's Day.

In those days our custom was to go early to town on Christmas business. I had carried a good heap of seaweed to the crest of the cliff above the strand, and was all set to start carrying it with the good ass I had, for it was a dry, windy day. I looked and saw a young lad coming towards me. I saw at once that he had some business with me.

'What brought you here, my boy?' said I.

'Your mother sent me to you to see if you would go to Dingle,' said he, 'for the whole village is going there.'

I thanked him and told him I'd go.

He went back home hot-foot.

'Tell my mother to have my clothes ready for me, and I'll bring you some sweets,' said I.

I started off after him without much enthusiasm, for all the hindrances were putting me wrong, and I hadn't carried my manure to the field, but since the whole Island was going to get ready for Christmas, I said to myself that I'd find it easier to go in their company, for I should have to go alone if I left it till later.

When I got to the house I was as pleased as anything, for I saw the old man had the ass ready.

'Where's the seaweed back there?' said he.

'The big heap,' I answered.

When I was ready I ran out, and all the men in the Island were on the cliff above the creek, all of them in their new clothes, one man with a sheep or two, another with a basket of fish, a third carrying a sack of wool, and all of them making for the boats to sail them up Dingle Bay and moor them at the quay.

My three uncles and my sister Kate's husband, Pats Heamish, were going down to the boat for Dingle. Though they were all good friends of mine, I wasn't too anxious to go in their company. I'd had enough of Pats Heamish the day I was with him, and of my uncle Diarmid, too, you may be sure, that day with the pigs, and that wasn't so long ago either.

When I came to a halt on the cliff-top, Diarmid came

from below after taking a basket of fish down to the water.

'Are you going to Dingle?' says he to me.

'I was thinking of it,' says I.

'Why on earth, then, couldn't you get ready?' said he. 'Have you got any fish or anything else to take with you.'

'I had half a hundred pollock to take, but I haven't the time now to put them together,' says I. 'Aren't you all ready now?'

'Run off with you now and put them up,' said he. 'The boat will wait for you.'

As I've said before, Diarmid was the best of the whole lot. The rest hadn't a thing to say to me, though all who were going in the boat were kinsmen of mine.

I sprang off at once. I put up my fish with two ropes I had. Another lad brought one of the bundles down to me, and I had the whole thing done in half an hour. The boat was afloat, ready and waiting for me. 'Holy Mary!' says Diarmid, 'you didn't take long.' They took the bundles aboard and off we sailed for Dingle.

In those days there were always women called 'hucksters' on the quay. Their business was to buy and sell fish, and they made their living out of it. When we had cleared everything out of the boat and carried it up, these women rushed at me, and before long they had bought my fish from me for fifty shillings the half-hundred.

'In Mary's name!' says Diarmid. 'You've got the price of a drink off the women pretty quick.'

'He has, my lad,' said a spirited woman of their company, 'and you'll get a drink too. Come on.'

As he had a great taste for it, he went along with me, and we entered the same house. The women paid me every penny, and when I had the money, I asked them what they'd have.

'Oh, you'll have a drink off us first,' said the woman again.

She called for a drink and paid for it on the nail. The second drink was on me, of course, as I was making money, and the third on Diarmid, for the women had bought his fish, too.

Diarmid and I had drunk three drinks by this, and as he always had a slate loose, you'd have sworn he'd been drinking for months. Off we went down to the slip where the boat was: we hadn't made it fast yet. We'd hardly got there when my uncle Tom called to me to go with him for a bit. He hadn't sold his two sheep yet.

'I'll come,' said I.

'Holy Mary!—you may as well secure the boat,' says Diarmid. 'It's late in the day and you'll be all over the town before morning, and maybe the tide will carry her away.'

'Your soul to the Big Fellow!' says Tom, 'you took good care not to worry about the boat before you'd done your business; and hold her tight now or let her go for good, you scamp!'

I've said already in this book that a gust of the ill wind had always been blowing against me ever since the day the poet and his songs kept me from cutting the turf, and just after that when the girls fell on me.

When one of my uncles called the other a scamp, anyone could see that that day would be no holiday for me to range at will, the more so as one of them who had little enough sense at the best of times had a drop taken. I was right, for in a minute Tom had got a coward's blow in the ear-hole.

That blow sent bold Tom off his feet and sent him flying over the sheep on the flat of his back, but, when he got his footing again, he went for Diarmid, and, if the fishwives hadn't been about, he'd have sent Diarmid into the other world and me after him, for, make no doubt,

I'd have died to save Diarmid, as I died—or all but—in the seals' cave.

When the battle was over, the first thing I did was to call the women in with me and give them another drop. Diarmid had escaped into another house farther on in the town by this, and I was glad enough to see him go. The women were dragging at my clothes, pressing another drink on me, but I didn't want to take two drinks in the one day off them. And I had another reason—I knew by the way they were going that my relations wouldn't have much sense to spare soon, and that it was just as well we shouldn't all of us go out of our wits, particularly in this holy season, in honour of which we had come upon that trip.

When I left the public-house with these ideas in my head, at the first glance I threw down the street in which I was, what should I see but my uncle Tom at grips with two skinny butchers who were trying to force his sheep from him for anything they liked to give him. I hurried up to them, and when I joined my uncle, he had gone all colours under Heaven. This affair hurt me sorely, and the two rascals didn't recognize me. They thought I was only a lad from the country. Tom had the sheep tied up with a new rope, and it had cut one of his hands as he struggled to hold back the sheep from going with that pair.

It was the worst bit of luck for the butchers when I came on the scene, for they thought that I was some young country rascal poking his nose in, and that I was on their side.

'Shift the rope out of your hand and give it to me,' said I to Tom. He did so at once.

'Stand up for me and the sheep now, and, if you've got as much spirit as you have strength, you surely won't make much account of these two damned scarecrows.'

I was angrier then, I think, than I had been since I came into the world, or have ever been since.

Tom set to work with his foot first, and the young butcher sprang to one side. The kick landed on one of the sheep and laid her out stone dead. We were in a fine hulla-balloo then. The butchers ran off. I had a knife in my pocket, and I rushed to the sheep and let out her blood. Now, if ever, my uncle wasn't pleased with himself: he had one sheep unsold and another was dead, and, another thing, a shilling meant more to him than a pound to my other two uncles. His heart was wrung; but the father of the young butchers found out what they had done, and he gave the same price for the dead sheep as for the living.

I left the sheep-dealer there and went off east along the street. I met with a man or two of my companions going about their business, getting through it with all speed, for they were in a hurry to be going home again, the day being fine.

I hadn't seen Liam yet or Pats Heamish, my sister Kate's husband. I found Liam in a public-house—Muirisín Bán's place. He was a real Irish friend to us. Liam had sold two sacks of wool, and had drunk enough and to spare.

'In with you and take a drop of this stuff,' says he to me. It was porter that he was gulping down as a cow drinks water.

'Serve him with a glass of whisky,' says he. 'I fancy he's no taste for this black stuff.'

The man behind the bar did so. There were five other men round Liam at this time, all talking together and drinking. I heard more talk outside, and I went over to the door to see what was there. What should I see but a couple of peelers taking a man to the jail; and when I looked closely at him, I saw that it was Pats Heamish. I turned round and told the man in the shop what I had seen.

'We can't get him out anyhow until ten to-night,' said he.

In all truth, I was nearly beside myself to hear that.

Our boat's crew were all in a hopeless mess by this, and the other boat's company ready to go home with a lovely evening for it.

I thank God to-day, as I did then, that I didn't do what I had in mind to do, and that is: sit down and drink my fill. I felt that if I did so the world would surely go as easily with me as with the others who were taking that line. I had good cause to be angry: the boat that had come out with us gone home, and the crew of my boat was melting like the foam on the river: three of the brothers sodden with drink, one of them in jail, and, as for the two others in the boat, I hadn't seen them all day up to now— the man we called 'Kerry' and the young lad of his kindred.

I went down to the quay, and at that very moment the other boat had just put to sea from the slip. They said farewell to me, and I sent my blessing with them. It was a lovely evening at this time, though the sky didn't look too promising.

When I turned back from the quay, whom should I see coming towards me from the town but Kerry, with a load of carded wool on his back.

'Where have you brought that wool from?' said I.

'From the carding mill,' said he.

I told him that the other boat had gone home.

'It has, has it?' said he. 'And sure, if it has, it won't get there. I suppose you've got all your stuff put together?'

'I haven't; and I haven't bought sixpennyworth.'

'Well, there's plenty of time yet. It's long enough till ten o'clock.'

'It looks as though you had no more shame than the rest of them,' I said to him. 'The other boat has gone home, and here we are still, and maybe it'll be a week from to-day before we can leave Dingle.'

'We shall be at home as soon as they are,' said he. 'Go in here and we'll have a drink, and we'll start packing up then and have everything ship-shape for starting back after the first Mass to-morrow.'

When I heard that speech, my mind changed, and with good reason—to hear such good sense from this man whom all the rest of the crew considered a useless ne'er-do-well, while they themselves were all crazy by this. We went in. We bought some goods, three of us, and, when we'd done, the shopkeeper stood us a drink. We went up the town then, and whom should we meet coming towards us but the prisoner, Pats Heamish.

'God and Mary to you,' says he.

Kerry returned the greeting. Pats's speech was still wandering. Muirisín Bán had got him out. I hadn't seen the three rakes yet. I left the three others there, and never stopped till I reached the house of our friend Muirisín Bán, where they generally spent their time. The three were there, and every syllable they let out of them would have split a head of brass. They were so dizzy with the drink that they hardly knew me till I spoke.

'Isn't that you?' says cracked Diarmid.

'I'm here,' said I to him. 'Are you in any better way now than when I left you a bit ago?'

'I am, my boy,' said he; 'isn't it a good way to be in to have a full belly? Have you seen Kerry and the other lad since morning?'

'I have, and he's not like you,' said I.

'Ah! devil take him; the lout never was like me.'

'Is the crew of the other boat ready yet?' says Tom.

'They're nearly half-way home by now,' I answered.

When Diarmid heard this, he put his head out at the door, looked up at the sky and the stars for a bit, and then came in again.

'In the name of the Virgin, young lad,' says he, 'that's

a boat that'll never come to harbour, to judge by the wild look of the sky up there.'

When I heard this from two men whom I knew to be good judges of the sea, I left the house where they were and started to visit the shops, where I wanted to spend a crown or a half-crown, for the shopkeepers are always wide awake at Christmas time to get a shilling or two. I never stopped till I had finished with them.

God forgive me! I went that round with the intention, if the next morning shouldn't prove fine, of going back by road and leaving the drinkers in their own company, for I was well aware that so long as they had a penny in their pockets they'd be long enough about packing up.

I hadn't had a bite since I left the house in the morning, nor had any of them. I found a house where I could get some food, and had a meal. When I came out again, the lamps were being lighted, and I went to look for my friends. They were all gathered together in the same house—the three uncles, Pats Heamish, Kerry, and the lad. Every one of them had a white bag open, and the shopman was stripped, weighing out tea, sugar, and everything else they wanted. They filled the bags up—one man with a stone of flour, another with a stone and a half, and a third with two stones. In those days we only took in a small store, and they bought all they wanted in this house.

Then we went out to the lodging-house. One of them took food for two who didn't. Kerry and the lad shared a bed with me, and we had only just lain down when the night blew up to wind and heavy rain.

'Do you hear that, my boy?' said Kerry. 'How far on do you think the boat is by now?'

'Somewhere near Ventry Harbour,' said I.

'If they're as far as that, they needn't grumble,' said he.

As the night went on, it grew wilder, and, though I didn't let on, I was terrified for the boat which had left me. And no wonder, for some others of my kin were in her, and, besides, even if I had no relations on board, a man is often worried about good neighbours. Before long the house was trembling, so that none of the three of us got a wink of sleep till the light grew in the east in the morning.

When the day was light enough to see anything, there was a lull in the wind, and it blew towards the land from the very point of the compass that we wanted to sail, straight from Dingle Quay to the Blasket Harbour. I flung myself out of bed and ran out at once into the street. I looked towards the four quarters of the sky. The sky was quiet now that it had got rid of its gathered fury, exactly like the drunkards who lay there in the lodging-house and had taken no notice of the wildness of the night or of the coming day either.

I ran in again and went to the place where I had slept, for half my clothes were still there, and I hadn't so much as gone down on my knees to thank God, who had saved me from the night's storm and had given us the blessed light of day so fair again.

'It's a fine day,' said I to Kerry.

The people of the house were astir at once, some of them meaning to go to first Mass. Kerry and the lad were the first two to come down, and he told me to wake up the rest. I told him that, whoever went to call them, it wouldn't be me. I had seen all I wanted of them yesterday, and didn't mean to spend to-day in the same manner. As the pair of us were conversing, who should come down the stairs but Pats Heamish.

'Morning, boys,' says he.

The man of the house it was who returned his greeting.

'How's the day?' says Pats.

'A fair wind home, my lads,' says the man of the house.

Pats turned back upstairs again to call up the rest and before long we were all gathered together. Diarmid ordered the woman of the house to have everything ready on the table for us when we returned from Mass. We should be hoisting sail on the *Black Boar* as soon as we had eaten.

The congregation was gathering for Mass, and, as soon as it was over, we ate our food and went out. We took all our things down to the harbour, ran the boat down, and threw everything aboard. We turned her stern to land and her prow to sea. Up went the sails, and we set out for the west with a fair following wind.

It took the *Black Boar* no time to make Ventry Harbour. As we were crossing the harbour mouth, one of the crew glanced at the sea between us and the land.

'There's a boat coming out to us,' he said.

I looked closely at her and recognized her sails at once.

'That's the boat that left Dingle last night,' said I.

We brought the *Black Boar* into the wind till the other came up level with us, and sure enough she it was. They told us all that had happened to them, and that all the goods in her weren't worth a crown, for the great sea had swept over them, and if it hadn't been that they had reached harbour before the storm came, not a man of them would ever have been seen again. We let the boats run side by side under their four sails, and we had a fair wind till we reached the harbour in the Blasket. Every woman, child, and babe was there waiting for us. The merchandise was all taken home, and we were telling tales of the town for a day or two.

I had five bottles of whisky with me—one from this man, another from that, and one that I had bought myself. That was easily done in those days. Half a crown a bottle was the price. The crews of the two boats had brought raisins, candles, and lots of sweet things from Dingle with them. There was plenty of turf for fire that year, and potatoes, too, and fish to eat with them.

I have already mentioned that I remembered the time

when there was only one pot-oven in this Island. There were three or four in this year I am speaking of, and, if there were, they had plenty to do.

Next morning my mother had one of these pot-ovens hard at work, for it was only a week to Christmas Eve, and she had four loaves to make for the household. We had only just finished cooking these loaves when in came uncle Diarmid. He had just been visiting the strand.

'My soul from the devil, my duds are falling off me, for I've had neither bite nor drop in my belly since I left Dingle,' says he.

I was sorry for him, and I went to a box I had and brought a bottle and a cup and handed him a drink. He tossed it off without drawing breath.

'Wisha, God send me something to repay you with!' says Diarmid.

'Put a drop of water on the fire,' said I to my mother, 'and make him a cup of tea and give him a hunk of the loaf. He made himself dizzy with drink in the town.'

'O, for God's sake, let me be,' says Diarmid. 'That cup has put me on the pig's back.'

Though a drop of drink had often before made much merriment, I had more fun out of that drop that I've ever had since.

The drink ran through every vein of him in a rush, for his skinny frame was as thin then as a conger that would have spent a week from Monday to Monday in a lobster-pot. I shouldn't have been so pleased with my bargain if it had been early in the day when I gave him the cup, for I should certainly have lost my day's work, and not I only, but everybody else who was in a position to see or hear him. It came pretty near to people declaring that he needed a strait waistcoat. I put my head out in the doorway, and who should be out there but one of Diarmid's boys, snivelling.

'What's wrong with you, Shaneen?' said I.

'I want my dad,' says he.

'O, come in, my lad. He's in here at the top of his form, thinking of marrying again. He's thinking of deserting your mother altogether. I suppose she's sent you to look for him?'

I spoke thus to the boy to cheer him up a bit, for he was the most pitiable object I'd ever seen. I took the lad by the hand and led him up to Diarmid.

'Is this boy yours?' I said to the rake.

He looked at him.

'Yes and no,' said he.

'We know no more than we did before,' I said to him.

'Yerra, my friend, don't you see that he doesn't take after me. He wouldn't have that tough swarthy hide if he'd taken after me instead of that swarthy simpleton of a mother of his.'

'I fancy,' said my mother, 'that none of them take after you. They're all like their mother.'

'Devil a one of them all in this village!' says Diarmid the joker.

I jumped up and gave the boy a slice of the loaf, and told him to run home. His father would spend a bit more of the night with us. I'd no sooner got rid of the boy than a woman came in through the door, and who should it be but my sister Kate. That gave my mother a great start, for she thought that there must be something wrong with one of the children, for she was only a very rare visitor with us.

'Something's brought you here to us so late as this,' said I to her.

'It's Pats Heamish who's not feeling very well. Since he left Dingle he's not had a bite to eat, and it's for a spoonful of whisky I've come,' says she.

'Didn't he bring a drop with him on his way back home?' said my mother.

'Wisha, not he, nor anything else,' says she.

'What should that fellow bring with him?' says Diarmid the cracked. 'He hadn't a blink of sense in Dingle from the time he left home till he got back again.'

'Madmen always plume themselves on their sense,' said I.

Kate was in a hurry. I went to the bottle. She had only brought a cup about the size of an eggshell for fear she would drive me out of the house by asking too much. I fetched a quarter-pint bottle and filled it up. She left me and hurried out of the door, full of thanks and blessings. I turned back again to Diarmid with the half-empty bottle.

'O, may it split me like a salmon if I taste it!' said he. 'I got enough in the one drink.'

I put a glass in my father's hand, and told him to hold it for me. I poured about half a glass into it. My mother did no more than just taste it. Then I filled up the glass for myself—the first taste since I left Dingle. I filled the glass again, and handed it to the joker.

'O,' said he, 'after swearing that oath!'

'Yerra, there's no meaning in that salmon, you fool,' said I. 'It's only an expression people use.'

'Wisha, by the Virgin, I fancy you're right,' says he, and tossed it off.

He stayed with us till it was high time for bed. My mother had never heard of the risk I ran for him in the seal cave until he drank this last glass, and the first thing she did when she heard was to go down on her knees and offer up thanks to God, who had preserved the pair of us. But my father didn't attach all that importance to the thing.

When we'd had our meal, I went out to inquire after Pats Heamish. I said to myself that I'd have a bit of fun with him, too. He wasn't far from the fire, and he had his coat thrown over his shoulders and his pipe in his mouth, though there was nothing but ashes in it. I asked him if he was on the mend.

'I am, and I'd never have been any good again but for that drop.'

'I fancy there's nothing in your pipe.'

'There isn't—and I've nothing to put in it either, Tom Crohan, my boy,' said Pats. 'I'm suffering very much from a glass of bad whisky I drank the day we went to Dingle.'

'I guess you had others inside you along with it.'

'O, I had five glasses drunk when they ran me in,' said Pats.

I left him there then, Pats, the devil's own (that's the best name I can give him); he'd come back home from Dingle without a scrap for his children but what they could beg; his health was knocked sideways, too, and, from the look of him, he wasn't likely to be well to-morrow or the day after that.

When I got back home I found my trumpeter still going full blast with no check on his flow of speech, no hoarseness in his talk, no weariness in his movements, his tongue never stumbling, and his appetite still unimpaired, so it seemed. My mother was ranging up and down the floor, setting the hearth to rights in preparation for bed.

'By the Virgin!' said he to her, 'you'd do better to get some bouncing girl for your son than be going up and down for ever like that for yourself.'

'Well, it isn't me that's keeping them from him,' says she. 'I'd rather he got one by morning. But I fancy they're not so easy got as all that.'

'Yerra, your soul from the devil! aren't there five women back in the Inish plying their spurs after him, and not a one of them knows which of them he'll give the wink to to take the road with him!'

And after all his trumpeting the whole night long, his

voice was just as clear, just as lively as that of a man on a platform beginning on his first sentence. I'd suspicioned what the rascal was up to, when I saw him coming to the house early in the evening, and guessed that he wouldn't leave the house till he'd started something of this kind, for there had been a lot of talk in the village all the year before about who'd marry and who wouldn't. Besides, I'd had a sort of idea ever since that time with the pigs earlier in the year that he and the old woman of the Inish were putting their heads together about the business, and probably he'd made her a promise that he would open up the affair.

So far as I was concerned, I wasn't ungrateful to him for his jabber just then, particularly if I had any reason to think that anything would come of it; for to speak the truth, that's where I myself would have made my choice at that time.

'Agh!' says my mother, taking up the talk again, 'he's full young yet and for some time to come.'

'Is he of age now?' says the rake.

'Twenty-two three days before this coming Christmas,' says she.

'Yerra, little woman, what was I but barely twenty when I got that swarthy lump of mine over there, and she wasn't much of a match,' says he.

'I imagine,' I said, in answer to him, 'that she was a better one than yourself. It's you that's the comfortless husband. Though you've been away from home, it's a long while since you brought back anything worth while to your poor wife, and you made a miserable waste of your money.'

'Yerra! alas for you, you fool! I'm far more of a boaster than a waster,' says cracked Diarmid.

'Clear off out of my sight in the name of God and the Virgin Mary!' said I to him. 'Or don't you think at all of your hovel or of going to bed, or are you at all afraid that the swarthy lump will go off and leave you?'

He grinned, and 'O!' says he, 'not much fear of that!'

I ran out with a box in which was a handful of potatoes for the ass. I threw down a sheaf of oats, too, for the cow and a calf that we had. My father told me to do this. This was his job, but the trumpeting of the fellow in the house had prevented him doing it that night. When I came back again, he was still standing in the middle of the house, demonstrating to the old couple that the young woman's help would be a great advantage to them, and that, so far as he could see, this girl from the Inish had excellent stuff in her. Though he spoke his speech like a simpleton, some part of his advice was calculated for his own profit. He'd have the whole house to himself, you see. The old woman of the house was his own sister, and this girl wouldn't be his enemy when he himself had got her for us, of course. Often enough in the past, and still to-day, a man has affected the simpleton for his own ends, and I had a strong suspicion that there was a spice of that sort of trickery in Diarmid that day.

I had to take him by the shoulder and run him out through the door. He turned back again into the house and said: 'I mean to kill a big wether on Christmas Eve, and you shall have half of it.'

Out he went through the door, and it was high time for bed by that.

15. *A Merry Christmas*

IT was the morning of Christmas Eve. 'I fancy that I may as well go and get a sheep,' said I to my mother.

'Don't go,' says she. 'Give windy Diarmid his chance. We shall find out whether he comes up to his trumpeting. If he kills that big sheep there'll be enough for the two houses in her, but I'm afraid he won't made good his swaggering.'

She had far less confidence in him than I had. I expected that he'd keep his promise, if he did lay the big sheep low. He was a finished butcher, for those brothers had a big household when they kept house together. And often enough had the joker put a knife in a fine sheep of their flock without anybody telling him to.

I strolled out late in the evening to look if the cows were coming down from the hill, and what should I see but the rascal coming to the house with half the big sheep on his back. Diarmid had split the sheep so cleanly in two that half the head was still sticking to half the body.

When he went in, he threw off his load.

'There's a joint for you, little woman, for the Holy Day,' says he.

'May this day a year hence find you and us all in prosperity and joy,' said she.

Just at that moment in I came. I looked at the present.

'Yerra, a blessing on your arms, good old uncle!' said I. 'You're a man of your word if anybody is.'

'Didn't I tell you that I'd do it?' said he. 'Sure, if it

hadn't been for you and the help of God, I shouldn't have been alive to kill it. It's in honour of God that I killed it, and to share it with you. I shall never forget the seals' cave!'

I turned away from him and went to the box. I took out one of the four bottles that remained there, and came up to him.

'There, you've earned this drink to-day if you ever did, Diarmid.'

'Mary Mother! wherever did you get it all?' says he.

'Didn't you get a bottle from your friends yourself?'

'Devil a one except one my old friend Muirisín Bán gave me.'

Well, I filled him a glass and a half, for that was the full of the vessel I held in my hand.

'O, King of the Angels! don't you know that my old skeleton can't take in all that at one gulp after the day's toil?'

'This is the little Christmas drink.'

He seized the glass, and before long all its contents were in a place that kept them safe, and he said directly:

'I hope with God that we shall have a good Christmas and a good Shrove to follow.'

Then he jumped up and ran out through the door.

I ran after him and brought him in again.

'Yerra, aren't you in a hurry?' said I.

'O!' says he, 'to-night isn't like other nights, and it isn't right for me to fail my own little crowd on God's Blessed Eve.'

I'd always thought that he wasn't so devout as he showed himself that day, for he was always a rough-tongued chap, and it was his constant habit to go seeking help from hell whenever he was in a rage. His expressions that day increased the respect I had for him. After a bit he went off.

When the time for lighting up came on 'God's Blessed Eve', if you were coming towards the village from the south-east—for that's the direction in which every door and window faces—and every kind of light is ablaze that night, you would imagine it a wing of some heavenly mansion, though it is set in the middle of the great sea. You would hear a noise in every house that night, for, however much or little drink comes to the Island, it is put aside for Christmas Eve. Maybe an old man would be singing who'd never lifted his voice for a year. As for the old women, they're always lilting away.

I felt that I would rather go out a bit than spend the whole evening at home. The place I meant to go to was Pats Heamish's house for a bit, for he wasn't too well yet. I knew that he hadn't got a drop of drink, so I got a half-pint. There was a score or so of welcomes waiting for me. He was a man you could get a great deal of sport óut of, but he was anything but happy, as he hadn't got a drop for Christmas. He'd drunk up all that he'd brought with him from Dingle, as his health had gone to pieces after the carouse.

I handed him the half-pint.

'Drink that down,' said I to him, 'for you've got to sing a song.'

'You'll get no song,' says Kate, 'if he once gets the half-pint down.'

'I'll sing a song, too,' says Tom.

He drank a tot and sang, not one song, but seven of them.

On Christmas Day and during the Christmas season we used to have hurley matches, and the whole village used to be mixed up in the game. Two men were chosen, one from each side, for captains. Each of them would call up man by man in turn until all who were on the strand were distributed in the two sides. We had hurleys and a ball.

The game was played on the White Strand without shoes or stockings, and we went in up to our necks whenever the ball went into the sea. Throughout the twelve days of Christmas time there wasn't a man able to drive his cow to the hill for the stiffness in his back and his bones; a pair or so would have a bruised foot, and another would be limping on one leg for a month.

That Christmas Day my two uncles, Diarmid and Tom, were on opposite sides. I was on Diarmid's side, and that's where I preferred to be, for, if I had chanced to be against him, I couldn't have put out half my strength if I had been anywhere near him.

We won three games from them, one after another, and the two sides were raging—they struggling to win one game, anyhow, in the day and the other side swaggering.

When we were approaching the cliff path on our way home, 'O, shame on you!' says uncle Diarmid, 'we didn't let you win a single game since morning.'

When Diarmid made that remark, his brother Tom was going up the path, just in front of him. He turned down, and, raising his fist, gave him a blow in the ear-hole that sent him down on to the strand a cold corpse or nearly.

'Sure, you little devil, it wasn't you that did it.'

He hadn't far to fall, but it was rough ground. He lost his speech, for it was knocked clean out of him, and it was an hour before he could talk, with all the others about him on the strand, all except the man who hit him—he'd gone home. Before long his feeble voice began to strengthen, and when it came back he made no good use of it, for the first thing he said was: 'On my body and soul, I swear I'll be the priest at that fellow's deathbed!'

They set him on his feet, and he wasn't long in coming to himself. He only had a scratch or two on his cheek. We went off home, and it was as much as we could do, we were so tired after the day.

We didn't do much after the great match on Christmas Day, but everyone was pretty well lamed; their feet and their bones were sore, but we had a week's rest till New Year's Day. Those whose hurleys were broken looked out new ones.

Very nearly all the hurleys on the strand came from Ventry parish. They were made of furze stems that had a crook in them, and the ball was made of stocking wool, sewn with a hempen thread. Often it would hit some tall fellow on the ankle, and he'd have no more use of his foot for that day. Whether I was strong or not, I didn't use my hurley clumsily. I happened to be on the outer edge of the game on New Year's Day, and I swiped the ball as hard as I could, and who should be in its way but my uncle Tom, and where should the ball hit him but on the knee-cap. It put his knee-cap out of joint.

'Good for your arm,' says Diarmid, the first voice I heard.

Diarmid thought that his brother was not so badly hurt, but, when he saw that he was, the merry note of his trumpeting dropped a bit. People had to support my uncle home, and Diarmid saw to it that he got there.

As I was returning to my house, who should follow me along the path but Diarmid, and you wouldn't have paid twopence for him after the tiring day. I waited till he came up with me.

'I've got a bit of a job still for you,' said I to him.

He didn't care what the job was, but went along with me.

My mother mentioned Tom's leg to him. Hadn't it got a bad knock, she said, and it would be useless all this year: the knee-cap's a bad place, and very often it doesn't ever go back at all.

'He'll make a fine cripple!' says Diarmid.

'Is that all the sympathy you have for him?' said my mother.

'It's only a week since he shed my blood for little provocation,' said Diarmid. 'Let him come to himself—though I'm sorry for the children.'

After they'd said this much I went to the box and fetched a good big bottle that was still unopened. When Diarmid saw it, he thought that it had fallen from Heaven. I gave him a glass, and he didn't refuse it, for he had no excuse to, and when it was down in the place that stood in need of it, he said:

'My soul from the devil! sure I should have been ready for burial this day if it hadn't been for whatever moved you to bring so much of it with you: I fancy it must have been Providence itself.'

'Agh! I got most of it as a gift, Diarmid,' said I.

'Your soul from the devil! wasn't I buying their goods before you were born, and they gave me little enough of it,' says he.

'I expect they see that you're failing, and that it wouldn't be of any advantage to them to bribe you to get anything out of you!'

'May God give them nothing, the pack of rascals!' said he.

When I had my uncle as I wanted him—and that was when the drink had called to life his feeble voice—I said that I would pay a visit to Pats Heamish. Though he wasn't yet free of the sickness he got in Dingle, he was in the hurley game every day; and he wasn't much good at it that Christmas—a thing you could never have said of him before that. I reflected that a noggin of whisky wouldn't last long, and that I should get its value in fun out of Pats, so I took it with me and went to the house. I was willing to share with Pats, for, if he'd had it, I should certainly have had my share of it.

After I'd been there for a while I said at last:

'There's neither song nor story in this house to-night,

and oughtn't there to be some sort of goings on on New Year's Eve?'

'The man of the house isn't feeling too well yet,' said Kate.

'I expect he feels the lack of his rights,' said I. 'If he had something to lighten his heart, maybe there'd be some sport or other going.'

'Devil a lie in that, Tomás Crohan,' said Pats, 'whatever pains we have in our bones besides.'

I ran to the cup that was hanging up on the dresser and brought it with me. I poured a mouthful into it and gave it to him. There was no need to press it on him, and before long he was singing 'Báb na gCraobh', and he went on from one song to another.

Soon I heard the noise of boots approaching, and I thought it was my father coming to call me in to a meal, but when he stuck his head in, who should it be but Diarmid.

'Your meal's ready,' said he to me. He had one of his boys with him who had come to summon him home, but Diarmid didn't want to go home at all, and what he did was to sit down on a stool with only three legs.

'Wisha!' says he, 'I suppose you don't know a verse of the "Súisín Bán"? It's a long time since I heard it.'

'Yerra, sorrow on your heart!' said I to him. 'Surely you won't stay to listen to that song when a boy has called you for your potatoes an hour ago.'

'God knows, if he sings it, I'll stay, and for another one after that, and till the light comes out of the east to-morrow,' said the lunatic. 'What is it to you? All you've got to do is to be off to your meal.'

Though he hadn't done what I said, I did what he said, and went out and left them there with not a thing in the wide world troubling the pair of them. When I got home, my potatoes were pretty well stone-cold.

'It's a pity you didn't stay a while longer,' said my mother, 'or did the rake give you a call?'

'He did, and the hound's outrun the messenger,' said I. 'He's there still.'

'Mary Virgin! isn't he the useless man,' said she.

When I had eaten my meal, the bee began to sting me again to go to the house where the fun was. I reflected that that night wouldn't come again till the end of another year.

Thinking so, I told my mother that I was going to Pats Heamish's house, and if I should be late in returning, not to worry over it.

'I wonder,' said I to the old couple, 'whether I'd better take a drop with me to Kate's house?' I was just trying it on with them to see what they'd make of it. I'd rather hear what my father had to say, for he'd never grumble at anybody unless he was doing something outrageous.

'Often has a man had a good drink in an enemy's house, and sure your own sister's house is not the house of an enemy: and if your uncle is there, too, isn't it all in the family?'

I went out at the door. I shouldn't have been at ease with my heart in it if the old couple weren't willing. I could hear the jester a long way from the house.

'Wisha! welcome here anyhow!' said he.

'Haven't you gone home yet?' said I.

'Devil a step!' said he. 'I have plenty of friends, God be thanked for it, all over the village. I make myself at home in lots of the houses. I've had my food here, my lad, and drink to go with it.'

'Have you had any singing since?'

'Yes, five songs: and now we'll have some more since you've come to us again. This is a night of our life, and we don't know who'll be alive when it returns again.'

I poured out a dram for them. Diarmid seized the cup and made to sing, and this was his song:

> '' *Tis the best of the doctor's prescriptions*
> *If whisky and porter are cheap,*
> *For it cures us of all our afflictions*
> *And puts all men's sorrows to sleep.*
> *And the old woman, wheezing and groaning,*
> *A-bed for a year in despair,*
> *When she sups her half-pint, stops her moaning,*
> *And kicks the bedclothes in the air.'*

All of us in the house shook his hand, seven times over, as no hand had ever been shaken before, when he'd finished the verse.

'You sing a song, Pats,' I said to the other man. He sang 'Eamonn Mágáine', and it delighted me, for he had a fine voice—that is to say, when he'd cleared his throat with the right stuff. Then the rake sang 'Cosa buidhe árda dearga'. He sprang to his feet, and 'Wisha,' said he, 'God's blessing on the souls of your dead, sing me "The Quilt". I've never heard the whole of it together since the poet Dunlevy let it out of his lips.'

I didn't require much pressing, though 'The Quilt' tried me hard. I sang eighteen verses of it.

'O, King of Glory! eternal praise be to Him! How on earth did he put it all together?' said Diarmid.

So we went on till the day lightened over us from the east. The day was breaking when we parted from one another.

'I pray God that no blot or blame may befall you till the year's end,' said Diarmid, facing eastwards to his own house. My way led west. I went to bed, and it was dinner time when I woke again.

The afternoon came on cold and stormy, and my father said to me:

'You'd better go up for the cows, since you've nothing else to do.'

I threw my coat over my shoulders and started up the hill. When I reached the place where the cows were, there were others before me there, and among them was the poet, with a stick in his hand, for he had a cow in those days whose like was never seen at a fair: a handsome, jet-black cow, that filled three firkins of butter every year that she was in good trim. He had a fine heifer, too.

'Well,' says I to myself, 'the poet shan't waste my day to-day as he did that day he met me, when he kept me from cutting the turf.'

We hadn't run across one another on the hill since then till now.

'Have you got any of the "Song of the Ass"'? said he to me.

'Part of it I've got, and part not,' said I.

'Have you got any paper in your pocket? If you have, out with it, and your pencil, too. I shall carry all the songs I ever made to the grave with me if you don't pick them up.'

I wasn't too pleased with what he said, for I didn't want to sit down by a tussock on a cold and chilly evening. But it wouldn't take the poet long to compose a verse on me that wouldn't do me any good! So all of us there threw ourselves down by a low fence, and my fine fellow started to sing his song.

I promise you, friend of my heart, that by the time I had a dozen verses written down that bitter, cold evening I wished heartily that the poet was dead, for, whoever found his ways easy to deal with, it wasn't me, and before I had the poem scribbled down on my paper it was black night.

Off we all started to go home. The cows had got there before us!

'Yerra,' says my mother, 'whatever kept you so long after the cows, a cold, stormy evening like this?'

I told her the truth.

'Well, the poet himself needed all the sense he has to stay out on a hill-top till now,' says she. 'Your food's cold now.'

I gulped down a dozen potatoes that were pretty cold, only that I had a drop of warm milk and some hot fish with them, and then I ran out again. There was a special house in the village that the young folk, boys and girls, used to gather in and stay till midnight. To give some account of that house and the young people that used to gather together in it, I am proud to be able to say that nothing wrong ever happened among them for the sixty-seven years that I've known it.

We spent the night sporting together till it was very late. Then I came home and went to bed.

16. *Shrovetide, 1878*

SHROVE came early that year (1878), and the Islanders
had to set about making their matches sooner than the
mainlanders, you see. So one pair set out quickly. I don't
think the matter of the dowry held them back very long,
for there wasn't any on either side.

When this party got as far as the priest's house, and it
was time for the marriage to begin, the girl couldn't be
found anywhere, dead or alive, though there was a crowd
hunting for her. A man from Dunquin who'd come to
Ballyferriter for another marriage told them that he had met
her on her way back. They sent a man on horseback to catch
up with her, but, when he got to Dunquin, she had set sail
for the Blasket in a boat that was going out fishing.

She hadn't been home many days when she started out
again with a man she preferred to the first one. Very few
people accompanied them, for they thought it rather an
odd proceeding. The girl had no one with her. Though
there wasn't a pin to choose between the two men, it's
plain the girl had some good reason for preferring one to
the other. The boy she'd jilted didn't leave his oars idle.
He went as far as Tralee for a wife—the daughter of a
Dunquin widow who was in service there.

I used to put up at the same farm-house in Dunquin as
this young fellow, for I had one or two relations there. It
happened that bad weather kept us out there after this
comic wedding I've just mentioned. For I had gone to
the marriage, and I was a near relation of the girl's, too,
though I didn't quarrel with her for doing what she did.

Before we got a chance to go home, the beauty from Tralee was in Dunquin.

Next morning the young fellow who'd been jilted came in at the door of the house where I was.

'I suppose,' he said, 'that you wouldn't care to go to Ballyferriter with me.' That's where the priest lived.

'Why do you think I wouldn't?' said I.

'O, because you've only just been there; and, besides, your relative and I didn't make a job of it together.'

'What's that to you so long as you get another wife?' said I.

'Wisha, on my baptism, maybe you're right! But I haven't got her yet,' said he.

When we got to Ballyferriter there was a great crowd there—men with a thirst, thimble-riggers, and merry-makers. When the Blasket couple came up for their marriage, their own company came with them. That's the time I made the acquaintance of the girl, and I give you my word, if she'd come from Dublin itself, she wouldn't have shamed the city.

The first place we went to after the chapel was the public-house, where there was a great uproar of drinking and dancing and singing, and every other sport that serves to pass the time. When it was getting on for ten o'clock the people were beginning to scatter. You would see a man going off supported between two others, and the woman that belonged to him following behind with a lot to say.

The two wedding parties came back home the same day. They had enough provisions of every sort with them for the whole Island, and all the people of the village revelled and made merry in the two houses. I doubt whether so many Irish songs were ever sung at any two weddings as at those two. Voices were never still till high noon on the morrow in the two houses. Only the girl from Tralee sang a song or two in English. Her father-in-law danced on a table, and they had to smear it with soap for him, as a lot of people had been dancing on it before him. He was a marvellous dancer, but he'd had a drop to drink, and he hadn't been capering long when he upset, but, all the same, he recovered his stand on the floor and finished the step as prettily as I've ever seen it done.

It's still the custom in the Blasket—as it always has been —that, if any of them start on anything, all the rest are eager to follow. Some years the whole Island gets married, and for seven years after that, there won't be a single wedding. I refer to this year of which I'm talking—for not a single boy or girl was unmarried by the time Shrove was over.

One night after I'd been out—and it was pretty late on in the night, too—whom should I find in the house when I came in but windy Diarmid, and his voice was going as loud as ever I'd heard it; he was getting at the old couple, explaining what an unhandy thing it'd be for them if they spent another year without a soul to help them—'and maybe two years,' says he; 'and I've got a proposal for you from the best girl that ever broke bread, the finest and the handsomest girl every way.'

They didn't break off the talk after I came in, and we kept it up till you'd have thought that everybody in the house was in complete agreement; though the whole affair was to be gone into again, for all the advisers were not present. Be that as it may, Diarmid went out, and he could have trodden on a shell-less egg without breaking it. He fancied that the bargain was sealed.

My sister Maura, who had been in America and who had come back home and married again, heard that Diarmid the rake had been in our house with a match on his hands, and she came to see if there was any truth in the story. We told her how things stood, and she didn't like the idea at all; she made it plain to the old couple what

AUTHOR *(right)* AND TRANSLATOR

FELT-ROOFED ISLAND HOUSE

a responsibility anyone was taking on himself if he didn't marry near home, but made an alliance with a family that lived a long way off and wouldn't be in a position to lend a hand on a rainy day.

She had herself marked down an excellent, knowledge-able girl, whose people lived in the village, so that they could lend us a hand when we needed it, and she went on to explain the whole affair to us, like a woman reciting a litany, till she had the whole lot of us as tame as a cat.

She'd always had a great hankering after her first husband's people, and his brother's daughter it was that she'd marked down for us. The girl she had such high praise for—and she deserved it—was a sister to the man who is the King of the Blasket to-day—though he hadn't got the title of King in those days or for long after. My sister Maura, who made the match, has been in the grave since December 1923. She was eighty when she died. May her soul inherit Heaven!

A week from that day we were married—Tomás Crohan and Maura Keane—in the last week of Shrove in the year 1878. There never was a day like it in Ballyferriter. There were four public-houses there, and we spent some time in all of them until it was very late in the day. The town was packed with people, for there were a lot of other couples being married. There were five fiddlers there, one in each bar, attracting people to himself, while another of them was not in any of the houses but out in the middle of the street, and he made more than the rest, for most of the people were in the street.

We had to leave Ballyferriter at last, just when the fun was at its height, but since the great sea was before us, and there were a lot of us to take across, we had to go.

Many of the mainlanders went in with us—relations of ours. There was singing in plenty, dancing, and all sorts of amusement, and food and drink enough and to spare, till high noon on the morrow. Then the mainlanders cleared off.

It was said that there hadn't been so many marriages for fifteen years. The rest of the year was given to hard work. It was a great year for fish. They weren't catching mackerel or lobsters, but other fish which they went after in the day-time in big boats with a seine net in each boat, and the farmers of the countryside bought the catch from them.

I had been frequenting school—whenever we could get one—until I was eighteen. They had no great need of me at home for all that time, as I had a married brother in the house. His wife died and left two children. My mother looked after them till they could go by themselves. My brother went to America. Then I had to leave school, for there was only my father at home. I had left school for three years when I married, at the age of twenty-two.

Till that day I had known little of the world's responsibilities, but from that time on they came upon me. Everything I had to do with changed from that day. Marriage makes a great change in a man's life. His disposition and his view of all sorts of things alters, and, above all, it whets his appetite to be up and doing in life. As the phrase goes, I used to fancy, up till then, that food was sent from Heaven to us.

I set to work with keenness. Away I went to the strand to get seaweed for manure so that we could have more potatoes to rear pigs on. We had two cows at this time. At daybreak, stripped of everything but my drawers, with a rake to gather the weed, out I'd go up to my neck in the sea; then I had to carry it up to the top of the cliff, carry it to the field and spread it. I had no tea or sugar in those days, only milk, bread, and fish. I would be as early on hill as on strand—now off to sea, now hunting seals, another time out in the big boat with a seine net. Each of these jobs had its own time. The seal chase was pretty dangerous. At a certain period of the year men would race one another to them. On one of these days there would be a heavy swell in Poll na Baise, and a man could only make his way into that cave by turning on his side and trying to swim in, or one must go into a sea-cleft and make a shift to kill the huge seals and fetch them out through that narrow opening. I've told already how one day I nearly lost my life when the rope had broken and my uncle was drowning.

Since the day of my marriage I was always trying my best to provide for my household and get my share of everything that was going. For a long time to come my father was a great help to me in the house and out.

Ten children were born to us, but they had no good fortune, God help us! The very first of them that we christened was only seven or eight years old when he fell over the cliff and was killed. From that time on they went as quickly as they came. Two died of measles, and every epidemic that came carried off one or other of them. Donal was drowned trying to save the lady off the White Strand. I had another fine lad helping me. Before long I lost him, too.

All these things were a sore trouble to the poor mother, and she, too, was taken from me. I was never blinded altogether till then. May God spare us the light of our eyes! She left a little babe, only I had a little girl grown up to take care of her; but she, too, was only just grown up when she heard the call like the rest. The girl who had brought her up married in Dunmore. She died, too, leaving seven children. I have only one boy left at home with me now. There is another in America. Such was the fate of my children. May God's blessing be with them—those of them that are in the grave—and with the poor woman whose heart broke for them.

17. *Work and Wandering*

THERE were seven seine boats in Dunquin in those days
and two fine big boats in the Blasket, and, though the
mainland tribe and the Island people were close of kin and
much intermarried, they were always at odds over the
fishing.

One day the boats from the two places were all gathered
at Inishtooshkert. The fish were shoaling in great num-
bers. The custom was that each pair of boats had the
right to shoot the nets in turn. Two boats had to attend to
the seine net every time it was shot, one boat paying it out
and the other keeping it out of danger. If there was fish in
the net, it was a slow business to get it into the boat, as the
weight of the fish and the run of the tide were always carrying it on to the rocks.

We had shot the net round the shoal, and, though the
tide was running wildly, our two boats handled the net so
smartly that it was out of danger before it had a chance to
run on the rocks, and there was enough fish in it to fill one
of the boats. That left the Dunquin people nothing to say,
and the captain of our boat signed to them to shoot their
net, or he would shoot his at once as soon as the seine was
cleared. Rather than let the Island boat have its second
shot, the Dunquin boat put its net out, and it hadn't been
out long when the run of the tide began to carry it on to
the rocks: there were crags and sharp points of rock waiting
for it, and a strong spring tide was running.

Before long the boat which had the end of the net let it go, and off they went, both boat and seine net, through the channel northwards. None of the other Dunquin boats followed her, for they were afraid to—that same channel wasn't a thing to play with at that moment.

'On my soul and body!' cried our captain, 'sure the boat from Coomeenole is lost. Get ready your oars,' said he to the Island boat, 'and we'll go to her assistance.'

They trimmed their oars at once, and away went the two boats through the sound to the north, and the swell was storming the sky. The boats were through the passage in two minutes, and when we came in sight of the other boat she hadn't gone under yet—but that was all there was to it: she was full of water, and they were bailing hard to keep her from sinking.

The seine net was still in the water, for the boat couldn't carry it. Our captain told us to take the net into our own boat until the other boat had been bailed out, and then to put it aboard her. When she was dry we put the net aboard.

We had a boatful of fish in the two boats. We had to tie the Dunquin boat to us with a rope, and then the two boats must tow her through the passage southwards, which she had been carried through northwards. Our captain cursed the Dunquin people again and again for deserting the boat, and he cursed the boat he had saved as well for shooting their net.

If I ever got a big job of work done any day, it wasn't the days when I was cutting turf, particularly so long as the poet lived, and was able to go on the hill. He was pitifully old at this time when he was herding the black cow on the mountain.

One day, when I was just getting down to my work on the south side of the Island—a warm day of sun and pleasantness—I'd been cutting for a bit, but not for long, when I heard a voice above me. I recognized it all right, and, may God forgive me, I'd no great hankering after its owner, not that I disliked him, but because he always turned my days into idle ones.

'Yerra, stop a bit, the day's long,' said the poet, who was coming from the north side of the hill at the moment when he spotted me.

'Do you see those rocks to the south?' said he. 'Those are the Skelligs. My father spent a day fighting in them once.'

'How did that come about?' said I. And if I lacked knowledge when I put the question, I didn't lack it long, for the poet was eager to tell the tale, lying there with his belly turned up to the sun:

'The young of the gannet are called "corraí", and, when they are in season, they are all fat. All the gannets hatch on the smallest of the Skelligs, and you never saw anything like the crowds of young birds there. A boat with a crew of twelve men used to be guarding the rock, well paid by the man who owned it. This time a boat set sail from Dunquin at night with eight men in her, my father among them, and they never rested till they got to the rock at day-break. They sprang up it and fell to gathering the birds into the boat at full speed; and it was easy to collect a load of them, for every single one of those young birds was as heavy as a fat goose.

'The captain stopped them then, saying that the boat was full enough and that they must go aboard and be making the best of their way home. So they did at once, and away they went, leaving the rock with their big boat full of fat birds, and they were in fine spirits for the ourney home.

'As they were turning the point of the rock to strike out into the bay, what should they see coming to meet them but the guard boat; they hadn't seen one another till that moment. The guard boat ran up along their gunwale at

once, and they commanded them to throw the birds into
their own boat in a jiffy; and even that wouldn't get them
off, for they must go with them as prisoners, and their boat,
too; and, if they didn't find a rope round their necks, they
would have no reason to complain!

'But the Dunquin men didn't throw the birds in to
them, and so one of the guards jumped on board and tied
a rope to the stern and they began to tow them swiftly and
strongly, them and their boat and their birds, towards the
land.

'They had gone on so for about a quarter of a mile when
a man in the bird boat suddenly jumped up and laid an
axe to the rope that was tied to the stern of his boat, and
that put the guards in a wild rage. They turned on the
other boat, and some of them sprang on board and they
fell to hitting at one another with oars and hatchets, and
any weapon they could find in the boat, till they bled one
another like a slaughtered ox.

'The bird boat won the fight, though it was twelve to
eight. The eight Dunquin men knocked the other crew
about till they couldn't stir hand or foot. They sprang into
the boat and plugged the rowlock holes, and towed them
out some distance into the bay, intending to leave them at
the sea's mercy, boat and all, so as to finish them altogether. There was a widow's son in the guard boat who had
never lifted hand or foot in the fight.

' "It's a shameful thing to send me to my death when
I never interfered with you,' said he.

'The captain of the other boat said to him: "If we set
the sail for you, do you think you could get home to shore
with it?" He said he could. Two men went on board and
set the sail to rights for him, and he faced her towards his
own landing-place.

'The Dunquin boat got back to its own harbour, its
crew cut and gashed and mangled, their boat full of fat

young gannets and they themselves not too easy in their minds.'

'And,' said I to the poet, 'have you any tale to tell of the Iveragh boat?'

'I have. The man they hoisted the sail for got her to shore. Two of them were dead, and the rest were sent into hospital. After that they were less keen on that sort of chase and the guard was taken off the rock, and those birds are no longer eaten in these days.'

He told this long tale fine and easy, without effort or haste. Then he said:

'Maybe we may as well do a little more cutting in the bog, it isn't long till dinner time.' And he sprang up and cleared off from me up the hill.

When I myself jumped up after he had gone and saw where the sun had got to, I was in a very bad temper—the best part of the day was spent and I hadn't yet cut three ass-loads of turf. Where was all the work I had promised myself I would do when I left the house in the morning? And another thought ran through my mind: was I myself fated beyond all the people in the Island to have all my time wasted by the poet?—for I never saw him frequenting any of the others, but only me. These thoughts made a great change in me, so that I determined the very next time he should run into me that I wouldn't speak a word to him, and then he'd have to leave me. But that is a plan that I never carried into action, and I'm glad of it.

At that time there wasn't a single canoe here or any of the gear to suit them, only big boats that were always managed by a crew of eight. Each boat carried a big, heavy seine net, with stones tied to the bottom of the net to sink it, and corks on the upper rope to keep the top of the net on the surface. There were little boats, too, used by old men and young lads for line fishing, and they would often be full of the sort of fish that is caught that way.

Somebody said one day that two of the Islanders had gone to a fair in Dingle, and that they had bought a canoe from a man when they were drunk. Before long we saw her coming, and we marvelled at her. The women whose husbands were in her began a long, soft, musical lament when they saw the quill of a boat that they were in. But two of the young lads went up to them and said:

'Yerra, keep your senses, couldn't two of us do the job for you just as well even if they are drowned?'

I never heard such a cursing as the two lads got from the two keening women, for they thought that it was for lack of sympathy they mocked them. I was near the women at this moment, and I had a good laugh at the boys' joke. Isn't it ready they were to take up with the two wailing women the very moment their husbands should have left them?

A day or two after this I went up the hill to fetch a load of turf, and what should I see but this very canoe, I thought, down below me, full of some objects which they were throwing into the sea. But I drove on and brought down the load of turf. But it wasn't the canoe the two men had brought at all, for that one was in the Island creek.

Nothing more happened till the evening, when the canoe came round the Gob from the south with four men in her, who carried her up the Island quay and began to inquire for lodgings. They had a few potatoes and 'kitchen' with them in a white bag. They found a house to put up in. They were from Dingle, and, of course, we knew them well.

They stayed in Pats Heamish's house, and they had brought their own food with them, intending only to spend a week at a time, as they had to go home with the catch. The things I had seen them throwing into the sea were pots to catch lobsters. The Blasket people were as strange to that sort of fishing tackle as any bank clerk at that time. Not much of the year had gone before there were four Dingle canoes fishing lobsters round the Blasket after this fashion. The Dingle fishermen took hundreds of pounds worth of lobsters from the waters round the Island before we had any notion how to make a shilling out of them. They fetched a pound the dozen, and, to make the story better, the dozen was easy got.

When the people found out how it was done the two who had bought the canoe put pots into her. They took another lad in with them. They fished for a year—the only boat from the Island—and made money. Next year off went the crews, racing one another to get canoes, and they were difficult to come by, for very few were being built. Every new one cost from eight to ten pounds. I went off like the rest to get one, and Pats Heamish went with me. We took another good fellow with us. I found a canoe easily enough, just built, in the hands of a relation of mine, and for eight pounds we brought it away with us. We had to go out again after withes to make the pots with, and we had had plenty of trouble by the time they were catching fish for us. We rubbed through the season and the fine weather with them, and we had ten pounds apiece after paying for the canoe.

Merchants from Dingle used to buy the lobsters from us in those days, and others of us used to send them to market on our own. They made an excellent fishery, for the seine fishing had failed by this.

When there were a dozen canoes fishing lobsters in this Island, people in England got to hear about it, and a company there sent a tank boat to serve the place. A tank boat is a boat or vessel which has a device to allow the sea to flow in and out in part of the hull to preserve the lobsters alive there.

Pats Heamish and I applied ourselves to the lobster fishing early and late. They fetched ten shillings a dozen for a good part of the year, and when they grew scarce the price was a shilling apiece. It went on like this for two or three years, and another company in England dispatched another ship to the Blasket which offered a shilling extra a dozen for them. The new man was the man for us, you may be sure, particularly as he raised the price. Half the canoes went to one and half to the other, so as to keep them going.

Lobsters were plentiful in those days. In a few years' time boats from France began to call, offering a shilling a fish all through the year. So they went on till there were five companies blowing their horns off the Blasket coast in quest of lobsters.

A few years went by like this, and the fishers didn't want for shillings, as the boats came to our very threshold with yellow gold on board to pay for the catch, however big the haul might be. Just at the time that these companies were sending their boats to us, the talk was beginning through-out Ireland about self-government, or Home Rule, as it is called in another language. I often told the fishermen that Home Rule had come to the Irish without their knowing it, and that the first beginning of it had been made in the Blasket now that the yellow gold of England and France was coming to our thresholds to purchase our fish, and we didn't give a curse for anybody.

Nobody knows how much gold and silver those ships left along the Kerry coast in those days; while in the rest of the year there were other merchants to buy mackerel and steamships were chartered by them to carry them fresh all over the world. One night in March I got five or six hundred May mackerel and brought them to the Dingle quay. We got four pounds a hundred for them.

So long as those ships were coming to the coast, no poor man wanted for a pound. Lobsters were to be caught every season. Shoals of fish swimming on the surface were to be caught at night in part of every year, and we did very well with them, for we had the big boats and all the tackle after the seine fishery had failed.

One of these years we had had a great haul overnight, and when we had cured the fish—great heaps of it—there was no sale for it in Dingle. A report ran through the countryside that there was a great demand for fish in Cahirsiveen, for it was scarce there. Then the crew of our boat began to stir one another up, arguing that we were a poor lot if we didn't load up our boat with it, set her sails, and be off with her southwards through Dingle Bay, for it was there we should sell our fish soonest.

Next Monday in the morning we filled up the *Black Boar* with salted mackerel—of fish that wasn't very large or coarse. We had a fair wind blowing to the south to fill our sails till we reached the lighthouse in the mouth of Valencia harbour, and from there on to Cahirsiveen.

When we reached the quay there, a crowd came to meet us. We wanted to find out if there were any buyers of fish in the place, and we were told that there were; some of them were on the spot. One of them started to offer for the fish, but the price he offered was less than our expectations. Another man came down the slip and welcomed us heartily. He had the manners and the way of a gentleman. He called us out of the boat and gave us a drink and bought all the fish in the boat for a crown the hundred, and brought us to his father's house in the middle of the town for a lodging. We had some food there, and then we handed over the fish to the man who had bought it, and when we had finished with one another and he had paid us, he stood us one drink after another and wouldn't take anything from us.

We found our lodgings again, and we asked the host by his leave would we have time to take a stroll through the town. He said that there was more than an hour and we should have plenty of time. Off went three of us in company, for the rest in the boat were well on in years and had no taste for sightseeing. We went into a fine shop where drink was to be had and looked round us there. After a bit we came out and spent some time amusing ourselves by walking up and down the street. When it was time for everybody to be going to his own place, we returned to our lodgings, and about half-way there, at a street corner, three women came up to us, the three most upstanding, the strongest and the handsomest women for shape and build that any of the three of us had ever seen.

One of us had a grey head—though not from age—and the women spoke to him. They spoke to him in difficult English at first, and he knew a little broken English, but he couldn't understand very much of it properly. The other man with us couldn't understand English at all, whether broken or perfect. The red-headed woman who was speaking to us was a good six feet high. She had a shock of hair, and was a fine woman. She was a fishwife and guessed that we followed the same trade, and she was forcing her acquaintance on us. Before long I heard her say to the grey-haired man:

'Come along, Blashket man, won't you have a drink?'

'I woint nat, mam,' says the poor, grey-haired man, for he didn't grasp what was happening very well, and in a flash he turned to bolt, and, as he turned, she gripped him by the back-piece of his vest and tore away that piece from top to bottom. The red-haired woman followed us to the threshold of our lodgings to return the back-piece of his vest to the grey-haired man, and the two of us were short of breath trying to keep up with our friend's wild rush as he fled from her.

We slept well that night, and when we saw the light of day and had eaten something, we went out again. The grey-haired man had no vest, but he bought a new one, and a back-piece for the one that was torn. We all bought novelties all over the city so that not a man of the boat's crew brought back to the Blasket a ha'penny of the price of the small mackerel. When we had all our traps gathered together, off we went on the homeward way.

When we got home we had to tell everything, and, as always happens, there was a scandalmonger in our company, and he felt bound to bring up the tale of the vest. He improved the tale for them, and he came near to setting the grey-haired man and his wife by the ears; and the rest of us didn't get off with whole skins either. Whatever price could be got for goods in Iveragh from that time on, the women of the Island were anything but keen to let their men go there to sell anything for some time to come. Idle talk sometimes causes great scandal.

It was not till long after that that we paid our next visit to Iveragh. A night of storm came, and the next morning one of the big boats had been swept away. It was our boat that had gone. There was a hue-and-cry all over the village. This was a heavy loss to us, for she was still a fine, new boat, and for some part of each year we used to make good catches in her. And now she was gone without a trace!

One day I had gone into Dingle. It was a Saturday. In those days foreign boats used to come overseas looking for May mackerel along these coasts, and their habit was to moor in the harbours from Saturday to Monday. They were in the Dingle harbour that day.

I went into a house, and there I heard a boy from one of these boats telling the man of the house that one of them had found a fine boat adrift that morning near the Skelligs completely undamaged, and that they had taken her in to the quay at Valencia and left her in charge of the priest of that island so that he could hand her over to her owners.

'Maybe it's your boat,' said the shopman to me.

'Maybe,' said I to him.

We described the boat to the youth, and he described it to us, and we made out that it really was the *Black Boar*.

I told the host to serve the best drink in the house to the foreigner who had brought me this good news. And the foreigner burst out laughing.

'Surely it isn't the man who's lost his little boat that ought to stand a drink to us who still have our boat and have done well this week! That drink is on me,' said he, and wouldn't hear a word against it.

When I went out I met a man from Dunquin with his horse and cart ready to go home, and I got a lift from him for myself and all the stuff I'd collected in the town. That was a kindness on his part, and I was very grateful to him for it. I stayed with him in Dunquin that night, and on Sunday morning the Island boats were out to Mass. I tell you when they heard that the boat was safe and sound across in Valencia they were surprised and delighted.

On Monday morning we went south with the other boat, eight of us, so that both boats should have a crew of four on the return journey. When we got across we made our way to the quay in Valencia Island, and there the boat was perfectly sound. One of the King's men came up to us, a coastguard, and put questions to us to find out if it was our boat. We said that it was, and asked him if she was ready for us to take away with us; if she was, we would take her at once, for the afternoon was fine for the passage north, and, if the sea should be at all rough against us, we had not enough men to take the two big boats. He said that he had no right over the boat, but was only looking after her; that she had been entrusted to the parish priest of the island and that we must see him.

The parish priest wasn't at home at all, and since this was the case, we had to take lodgings in Cahirsiveen that night. We found the house in which we had been before.

The old couple in the house made us welcome. Believe me, or take the tip of the ear off me, that we didn't go strolling much about the town after the lights were lit that night.

When we had made ourselves ship-shape in the morning, a drink was the first thing to warm our hearts; the next thing was a meal, and we took things as lightly and easily as though we were in the Blasket Harbour.

' 'Pon your souls and bodies!' says the captain. 'Is it that you are without a care in the world on you? When shall we have this old hulk of a boat in harbour in the Island?'

It was a mischief-maker, no doubt, who gave him his answer and said:

'This is one of the days of our life, and maybe the last day we shall spend in this town of Cahir.'

When we came to Valencia the parish priest was waiting for us, instead of our having to wait for the priest. We greeted one another, and he questioned us about the boat, and then handed her over to us to take home.

We couldn't be satisfied then without finding a bar to drink *deoch-a-dorish*[1] in, and that was a long and lagging drink. The mischief-maker was the first cause of it, but another man stood a drink after him, and then another and another, and, to make a long story short, we stayed there till night.

There was Dingle Bay to be crossed, and we were not strong enough for the two big boats unless we had a following wind, and that we hadn't got. For one that was in a condition to do his job, there were two that weren't. At last we agreed to wait till the morning and the early part of the day anyhow. The host made room for us, and that suited us well. The next day was a feast day. There would be Mass at ten o'clock, and we should have the long day before us after that. In the morning when we had had some

[1] Stirrup-cup.

food we went back through the island, for the chapel is in
the middle of Valencia Island. We got there early, taking
notice of everything that came our way. Some of the
people there have large holdings—in the best part of the
island, you may be sure. These are the foreigners. The rest
have little land, and that in the worst part.

We got to the chapel like this, putting questions to a lad
from the quay who was in our company. It was an old
chapel, with four gables, and not very high or big. Two
public-houses faced it.

When the congregation was collected they were all very
neatly dressed, and though it was an island you would
have thought that they had been brought up in the centre
of the country. And as for clean, respectable clothes, those
were the sort they wore. When we went into the chapel,
the central part of it was open up to the rafters, while the
rest of it was covered with a loft on the inside of each gable.
Whether I said few or many prayers, they didn't prevent
me from casting an eye on the congregation, and I didn't
see a swarthy skin or a black-haired head among them in
the chapel or out.

We gave the inns the go-by when Mass was over and
started off back across the island; for we meant to go home
though the day was pretty rough and gusty by this. We
went into a farmer's house and got some milk to drink
there. We said to one another then that we had best go
where we could get a sight of the sea to the north, and we
cast an eye over it to see what it was like, and whether it
was too wild for us to make a course across.

When we went to the top of a round-topped hill there
we came on the big slate quarry that is there on the flank
of the hill. It was a wonderful sight for us. Coming down
from the quarry we had a fine view of the place of that
nobleman, the Knight of Kerry. He was often called the
Knight of Glenleem, for his residence is here in Glenleem.

We had had no experience of places of this kind, and it is little wonder that we marvelled at it.

At that time of day in Valencia Harbour there was the greatest sight of masts any of us had ever seen. All these masts were on big ships or little vessels, for fishing boats had collected there from far and near that year after mackerel. Plenty of money was being made, and the poor themselves didn't want for a pound. The upshot was that, by the time we got to the quay, we had pretty well wasted the day looking at this and that. That did us no harm anyhow, for the day was settling. Though it had been very wild in the morning, there wasn't a breath of wind out of the sky by this time.

We ran down to the boats so and set them afloat and gathered all the traps that belonged to them into them. At that moment the mischief-maker, who was always in our company, spoke and said that poor men ought to quench their thirst before venturing into the bay to the north.

Another man answered and said that maybe the crew hadn't much money in their pockets.

'Sure it's a poor pocket that hasn't anything in it,' says the mischief-maker. 'I'll stand you a drink myself,' says he.

There was nothing else to be done but to go with him.

We went. He called for a gallon of porter. When the man who was standing the drinks looked round, there was one of the eight who wasn't in the house, and he sent a man to find out where he was. He was in one of the boats lying by the quay. As he hadn't got a shilling of his own, he was shy of going with the company, and the messenger was hard put to it to fetch him along.

At last all our thirst was quenched, and we started for the boat. We said farewell, with a blessing, to those who were on the quay that fair and lovely evening of holyday. We set the boats' sterns to land and their prows to sea, as the mighty heroes used to do in the old days, and started out through the channel. The lamp was just lighted in the lighthouse as we were leaving the harbour. Off went our two boats racing together till we reached the landing-place in the Western Island, as we call the Blasket. As the night was short and fine, and we were in no haste or hurry, it was day by the time we got to our houses.

18. *An End to Boats and Middlemen*

ABOUT three years after the boats had been brought from Valencia we took them both with us to Dingle, full of everything likely to bring in money—wool, pigs, sheep, fish, and so on. They had a big cargo, and sixteen men to work them. We had a fine following wind east through the bay till we reached the quay and the landing-place in Dingle. The boats were put in safety, the crew sold all their goods, and then there was the night to spend in the town.

If that was a merry night for us, it was followed by a sorrowful noon on the morrow, for, when we went to the boats there were strangers in charge of them who wouldn't let us touch them—police who had authority to keep them from us. They had orders from the rent collectors, and, as we were not paying the rent in any other way, there was little fear that it would be paid now when we were cut off from our boats, our road through the sea, and our livelihood.

It was the talk of all Dingle—the Blasket Islanders imprisoned in the town. A number of people came from the countryside to see the wonder, and a friend or two with a trifle of money in his pocket to help us to redeem the boats.

The whole rent of the Island was demanded before there was any chance of freeing the boats, though there were many in the Island who had nothing to do with them. Two friends of mine from the country came to me offering money to redeem my share in the boats, but I refused it with thanks, for I saw no sign that they intended to let them go yet anyhow.

We wandered up and down the streets, and a kind shopman here and there offered us money if we intended to redeem the boats; but none of us would take it: we said that if there was any idea of redeeming them, we would come back to them. And we spent another night in Dingle.

Next morning we were in gloom and misery, without any change or advance in our troubles any more than the day before. We stayed there till midday. Then we were at the end of our patience, and the sixteen of us set out from the town, breathing rage and consigning all the middlemen and landlords to the black devils. We reached Dunquin, some of us getting lifts, but most of us going on foot. We had to hire a cart to carry back whatever goods we had bought. We had spent a little money on our journey, but we were forced to put up with it and keep on until we returned to the place we had left.

We were left with no big boats then, and ever since until to-day, only canoes. The rent collectors were beside themselves, for, when the boats had been put up for sale, they couldn't find a purchaser to pay a pound for the lot, and they had to put them into a field till the moths ate them, and they never got sixpence or a penny for them. That broke the courage of the bailiffs and the rent collectors from that time on, as far as the Island went. Since they didn't get a thing out of the boats that time, it was long before any rent at all was demanded of us; and the upshot of the whole affair was that you wouldn't find it hard to reckon up all the rent we've paid from that day.

We had to take to the canoes then and do our best to fish the sea with them by day and night—lobsters by day from

Mayday to August, and mackerel by night, every night that came fine when the fish were there.

We spent a few years like this, with more strangers coming for the fish every year till there were five companies at last after them, and there was a demand for the mackerel, too. So, if it was a cruel and toilsome job to come by catches of this kind, those who were taken up with this business never knew privation or hunger. If we had been as careful of the pounds in those days as we have been for some years past, it is my belief that poverty wouldn't have come upon us so soon.

Soon after this there came a change in the world, and not in one way only. The middleman had to give up the land, and shortly after a man came to the Blasket sent by the Earl of Cork himself. At that time the rent was at the rate of two pounds per cow—that is, eighty pounds on the whole Island—and this man summoned the Islanders together to come to some sort of agreement as to how much they thought they could possibly pay—that was the sum of his business with them.

After they had spent some time thinking it over, a rake there spoke at last and said:

'My soul from the devil! if I'd consider it worth my while to put a spade in earth unless I paid at the rate of a pound a cow for it!'

If there wasn't laughter over the rascal's speech, it isn't day yet; even the gentleman laughed. They understood the poor fellow to mean that he would feel himself in God's Heaven if he held his piece of land at the pound rate, considering that his father before him paid five pounds a cow, and often enough they had to pay more even than the five pounds, for the scoundrels used to be confiscating cattle every day from anybody who had them, for in those days they didn't give a rush for the law itself, and the poor had no means of taking up a case against them.

Whatever rent there was on the land after this, there was some improvement. We were done with bailiffs and injustice from that out. When once your rent was paid, no second demand could be made for it until the right time came round again.

We passed the time like that for a good space, and the Islanders were well satisfied with the arrangement, though the rascal who suggested the rent of a pound a cow got a jab or two now and again, as they thought that they could have got it for ten shillings just as well. However, they never felt the price of anything at that time, so long as a dozen lobsters fetched ten shillings, and a hundred of mackerel a pound; there was a plentiful supply and a constant demand. I remember a tank boat coming from England with three hundred pounds of yellow gold on board, paying a shilling a fish that day—and the three hundred pounds wasn't enough to pay for the fish.

People say that the wheel is always turning, and that's a true saying, for in the part of the world that I have known it has turned many times; and if the world improved a bit round the Blaskets at that time, and God gave us that much good fortune, I fancy we didn't take the care we should have done of it, for 'easy come, easy go' is always the way.

Looking round me in this year (1888) I found I had a little field of rough land in the upper part of my holding, and I determined to break it up, for it was very old land and useless as it was, and in my enthusiasm I purposed to break in half of it that year and the other half the year after.

Often a man has made an unprofitable plan, though at other times it doesn't turn out like that. This plan of mine wasn't worth much, for it resulted in a great deal of labour for me, and I gained little from all my work. I must set my face to the strand to get weed for manure; I had an old black ass, and he had to travel a mile and a half under every load, every step of it uphill.

Well, often has a man taken on a job, and before he'd had it long in hand he's found that he's had enough of it, and certainly that was the way with me. Very soon I was sick of it, more particularly as the old black ass was letting me down.

In the end I set half of the little field with potatoes. When I was planting them my father was in good trim; he was seventy years of age, and all that was wrong with him was that he was a bit bent. However, he used to pay a visit to this field every day, though he was getting weaker and slower every day.

Before long he began to give up his visits to the field altogether, though he was keen enough about it at first. One day, when I imagined he was in the field, I looked out and I couldn't see a sign of him there, and that struck me as odd. I asked a lad who was going by for news of him, and he said that he was in the house of Kate, his daughter, and sure enough there I found him.

'Father,' I said to him, 'wasn't I thinking that it was in the little field you were since you had your morning meal?'

'I don't hanker after it much,' said he.

'But you had a great fancy for it at first.'

'I had, but I don't feel like that now. I shan't see a potato come up in that field.'

There are many things we don't heed until it's too late. And after my father was buried I regretted that I hadn't questioned him and asked him whether he had seen or heard anything in the field when he visited it. No doubt, something of the kind happened to him, considering that he dated his life's end so accurately.

My father was in the grave before the potatoes showed above the ground. That left more of the world's trouble on poor Tomás; and that wasn't the end of my troubles either.

Round about Mayday there were mackerel to be caught that year, and we made a good penny out of them. I had five pounds put by at the end of a single week. Then my father died, and I had to take my five pounds and coffin him with them. Coffins weren't as dear in those days as they are to-day. The whole funeral cost about ten pounds then. It has often cost thirty pounds since then.

After I had gone through all this I had to wring more work out of my bones, and after all my toil working the little field there weren't two sackfuls of potatoes in it; only I got three crops of oats from it and the last crop was the best of them.

I set about the other side of the little field the next year, and I made a great deal more profit out of this half than out of the other that I had broken up first, for I had more experience of the nature of the soil, and I arranged my manuring to suit it.

There were ten sacks in this half of the field, and oats, too, for three years, for I paid more attention to it, as my eyes had been opened by my experience of the other half. Another thing, too, many a neighbour soul gave me his blessing, for I often reached my hand out to them when they wanted seed.

A short while after this my mother began to fail and to bid this world farewell, being eighty-two years old now. She had no cramp in hand or foot at that age, and she stood as straight as ever she did in the days of her youth. She was not ill long once she had been taken sick, and maybe it was as well for her to be done with the world then; and I had small chance to look after her then, the affairs of the world were so thick upon me. One night she was very bad and I had decided to stay up with her, when who should come in to me but uncle Diarmid, and he told us all to go to bed at once; he it was who would tend on the sick woman till morning.

Before the dawn came he called out: 'She's in the next world.'

I set about getting myself ready to face for Dingle to get the furnishings for the funeral. The weather stayed fine till my mother reached her family churchyard in Ventry—a long journey by sea and land from the Blasket, and, although there was a fine following of many horse-drawn cars, it was on men's shoulders that she went to her grave.

So ended the two who put the sound of the Gaelic language in my ears the first day. The blessing of God be with their souls!

19. *The Little Canoe*

A WHILE after this my brother Pats came over from America to me. I was amazed at his coming over this second time, for his two sons were grown up by this; and I fancied they were on the pig's back since they were on the other side. When I saw my brother after his return, anybody would have conjectured from his ways that it was in the woods he had spent his time in America. He was hardly clothed; he had an ill appearance; there wasn't a red farthing in his pocket; and two of his friends in America paid for his passage across with their own money. Though he hadn't had a day out of work all those long years he had spent every penny of his pay on his two sons; he wouldn't let them go to work, and any sixpence that was left over when he had paid the expenses of the three of them, it was his way to go to a bar and drink it up—and I fancy that it was little enough that he had to drink with.

I don't mean to spend much of my story talking about them, but will make a clean sweep of them and their fortunes: how they dealt with the father who had worked for them all those years, spending his sweat in the States of America trying to make men of them, to bring them up to man's years—and succeeding. The sum of the whole matter is that not a one of those two has ever asked after him since.

I knew my brother's mind and manners well enough beforehand, and though that was so, what was I to do?

I couldn't send the only brother I had adrift after he had come back from America. The fact is it was as much as he could do to keep in his right wits, and, if it hadn't been so, he wouldn't have had to depend on anybody, for he was the best worker to be found wherever he went. But where will you find a wise man without his weak side?

Well, just at this time there was fine fishing to be had round the Blaskets—mackerel and lobsters—and a great demand for them, and when I saw that Paddy was minded to help me, I thought the best thing I could do was to invent some way to put him to use.

The plan I fixed on was to take an old canoe that I had and cut it down so that it would be easy for two to carry it up and down, for most of the canoes at that time had only a crew of two for the lobster fishing in the season. We used to have a score of pots in the little canoe, and it would have delighted your heart to watch us fighting the sea with her, and I tell you that we did well at the fishing, though we never went far from home. We used to work round Beginish, and so we managed to get home for the three meals of the day. Others of the canoes used to go far afield, as far away as the Teeraght, Inishtooshkert, Inish na Bró, and Inishvickillaun—all the Lesser Blaskets.

The crews that went far afield like this had to take provisions with them every day and stay out from the dark of morning till the dark of night, and they were pretty tired by the day's end. No doubt the lobsters were far more plentiful in those islands than near home, though the home-worker drew level with them, for he visited his pots more often.

We sold many a pound's worth to the vessels that plied north and south through the Sound of the Great Blasket. They would have their 'speckled snowy sails' set, and often there wasn't a breath of wind out of the sky. We often

SCHOOLCHILDREN

APPROACHING THE ISLAND FROM THE MAINLAND

had our dinner on board, and we used to give them crabs and other small fish: they would give us tobacco and other things, and a glass of whisky for me—Pats never tasted a drop after he had left America, for he had bought his sense.

One fine day there came to us through the Sound from the south a small steamship towing another ship after her that had only sails, and was painted every colour under heaven. The sailing ship was black with people, every one of them looking more of a gentleman than his fellows as far as dress and ribbons went. The two ships were travelling slowly so that they could look at our Blaskets in comfort.

It happened that I was hauling up a pot near them at this moment, and what should be in it but a blue lobster and a crayfish, just as the two ships were passing by us on their way north. I held up the crayfish in one hand and the lobster in the other, and no sooner had I done that than every soul in the ships on deck, man and woman, was beckoning to us, and they stopped short on the surface of the sea till we came up to them. Nobody was ever welcomed like the two old fishermen. We had a dozen lobsters and two dozen crabs and three dozen of other fish, and the gentry didn't worry about how we looked, or our little canoe; all they thought about was to get fresh fish from us. One of the crew lowered a bucket to take up the lobsters, and when I looked at the bucket I fancied that he wouldn't have put a lobster in it for five pounds—it was such a fine vessel! He lowered it again to take up the crabs, and a third time for the other fish.

When he had collected all the contents of the little canoe on deck, he lowered the bucket again without a moment's delay, and, upon my oath, I thought that it was a hunk of bread that we had in the stern of the canoe that he wanted this time. But it wasn't as I thought, for, when I caught it in my hand and looked at it, what was to be seen in it was money. The man who lowered it to me spoke in English and said that there was a shilling for every fish I had sent up to him in the bucket. My gentleman drew the bucket up again, and before long I saw it coming down to me again, heaped up and running over, and the greatest lady of all on board was letting it down this time, so I thought, and she was the finest woman for manners and beauty that I ever saw. The bucket was crammed with every kind of food and 'kitchen', and I couldn't put a name to half of them. When I had emptied it in the stern of the boat, I doffed my cap and bowed to the lady, thanking her.

Soon a man came to the waist of the ship and told me to hand him the empty bottle we had in the boat. I did so, and before long he sent it down full of clear water, and asked me again whether we had another bottle in the boat. We hadn't. He left me again, and when he came back he had a splendid bottle with him that would hold about six glasses. He handed it down and told me to use a good deal of water with a little of the contents of the other bottle.

We said farewell to one another with a blessing. By this time we were a mile and a half from land. That wasn't far, for the day was fine. We had not parted with one another for long when my ill fortune prompted me to try what was in that bottle. The other man said that I'd better have sense and move in to the land first before I tasted it, and that I had plenty of time for it.

It was no good talking to me. I said that all I wanted to do was to taste it to see what sort of drink it was. I thought that, unless it was some special sort of poison, I should be safe enough with it; but, as with everything else, a poor sinner can't do what is best for himself. It was the little wooden cup that we used for the bailer that I took, and I poured about a spoonful, I thought, out of the bottle.

When Pats saw how little I had poured out, he said: 'Since you are at it, what's the good of a trifle?'

'Try the river before you venture into the current,' said I, like a wise man. And that's the last word he got out of me for two hours after that. We'd gone about a mile of the way by this, and there was another half-mile to go, and, to cap all, there was a gust of wind blowing, working up to a flurry, white with foam. That much I had seen before I drank the stuff in the cup.

Down it went. When I had drunk it, I stood a moment —so Pats told me afterwards—and then fell flat in the bottom of the canoe. The poor fellow thought I was dead, and fancied that there must have been poison in the bottle, and that the gentry had given it me by mistake. The poor chap worked the very stuff and marrow out of his bones struggling to make the land. Just after he had got there, at his last gasp, to a sheltered pool inside a creek in Beginish, that's when I came out of my swoon, with no hurt or harm.

'Maybe you'd better take another little drop of it!' said Pats to me.

I realized that it was disgust made him say that, and I kept quiet. Indeed, I was ashamed enough when I saw what a gale was blowing outside, and understood what a hard time he had had of it trying to make the creek with the little canoe, with me lying a dead weight in the bottom of it.

The gale was still raging, with no sign of settling; but all the same we had the shelter of the land now, and, to be sure, we weren't an unprovisioned boat at that moment. Though we were by Beginish—and that wasn't far from home—we had no thought of leaving the creek where we were.

After a while the gale went down a bit, so that Pats said:

'Perhaps we might manage to lift the pots? There's a lull in the wind by these rocks.'

I wasn't very keen to do it, but he was a man who liked to have attention paid to what he said, and when you crossed him, he'd be no use for three days to come.

We set about doing what he proposed. Most of the work fell on himself, for he was doing the rowing, while I was lifting the pots. We'd only just lifted them when the gale blew the crests clean off the waves. We managed to make the creek again. We got a dozen lobsters out of the pots.

It was midnight by the time we reached the Island that night, and our people were in a terrible state of mind, going round to get help to go and look for us, for they were sure we were drowned.

That was a great year for fish. At every shift of the pots you would get a dozen lobsters, and that meant a dozen shillings: those twelve shillings bought a half-sack of flour, and eight shillings a half-sack of meal, and so with everything else. A poor man could live easily enough in those days.

After those ships had gone from me there came an exceptionally fine month, without a ripple on the sea anywhere, and that was the sort of weather that was best for catching the fish that were going; and, what was even better, there was a great call for any fish you had. Pats and I were doing very well with the little canoe, for we had all the range we wanted, and there was nobody to interfere with us. The lobsters come into the pots best in the late evening. One evening we were very late, and they were going in thick and fast.

'It's a great shame for anyone to go home on a calm, peaceful night that isn't long or chilly,' says Pats to me, 'when there's gold to be got in the pots. If the folk of this place had been where I was for a while, they'd have a bit more knowledge.'

'Before we get home now it'll be day again,' says he. 'Let's leave the pots a bit and there'll be as much again in them as we've got out of them already, and, if that's so, isn't it a pity to leave them there.'

Now, he was the kind of man that, if you didn't give him his head, wouldn't go with you to-morrow, however much you needed him; and so, though I wasn't too pleased with the idea, I had to fall in with him, or I should have had to work the little canoe alone the next day.

'Come along,' says he, 'we've given them time enough; we'll have a look at them.'

So we did. When we drew up the first pot, you never heard such a row as was going on in it.

'I fancy there's a conger in it,' says Pats, who was at the oars in the bow.

'No, I don't think so.'

I thrust my hand down into the pot and drew out a fine lobster, and another one after him.

'Are there two in it?' says the man in the prow.

'There are. Two fine ones, too,' said I to him.

'That's two shillings. O, God of the Miracles! how I should have had to sweat in America to make two shillings, and all I have to do here is to pull up a pot through two fathoms of water!'

When we'd finished drawing the pots, there were a dozen splendid lobsters in them.

'Mary Virgin! how many easy shillings there are in the sea!' says he. 'When you think of other places where you have to sweat blood to make a shilling! 'Pon my soul and body, there are people in America who, if they could come by money as easily as this, would never slumber or sleep. They'd be pulling up all the time.'

I believed him well enough so far as that went, though he blethered a lot generally, and I often had some difficulty in believing him. I wasn't so ignorant that I

N

couldn't understand how it was in countries overseas—hard work, and the ganger spying on you, two of them sometimes.

We waited about an hour when I saw him putting out his oars again.

'It looks as though we were going to sleep altogether. Since we are spending the night out, we may as well have something for it,' says he, throwing into the sea one of the pot ropes in the bow which anchored the canoe while we were at rest.

As I've said already, I had to act as his servant instead of being the master, or we'd never have got anything done. We started to work again, and when we'd finished with the pots, we had another dozen. We anchored again.

'No wonder there are so many poor wretches on the coasts of Ireland,' says Pats, 'as indeed there are, and may there be more of them! For they deserve to be—such a crowd of lazy devils, snoring away at this time on a fine calm night, when there's gold and silver to be made for a little trouble and sweat.'

You might think there was something in what he said. Still you have to consider that a poor sinner can't keep at it night and day alike.

We stopped for a bit. I fancy that I dropped off into a doze. He said I did, and that I had a good bout of sleep.

'I think the grey glimmer of dawn is coming and that we'd best take another turn out of the pots, and then we'll get home, and not a soul will know how we've spent the night,' says Pats, throwing off the rope and putting out his oars.

I promise you I wasn't so lively by this time—the morning was beginning to peer then. I had an empty belly and was all numb and chill, whatever was the case with the man in the prow. But I pulled myself together, since I had to, and by the time we had the pots drawn, I was broad awake, and we had a dozen more lobsters, and two on the top of that.

When we turned our faces home, what should we see but a vessel coming to anchor, and it was plain that it was a stranger. She was in the Sound in front of us, and it wouldn't take us out of our way to go and have a word with her. When we came alongside we saw her name—*The Shamrock*. She had a tank for lobsters inside her, and it was lobsters she was after. They asked us how many lobsters we had, and how much we wanted for them. We told the captain that we hadn't much on board, but that we had as much again in a store pot over there. Moreover, we wouldn't ask more of him than we would off any other ship.

'Off with you, then, and bring all you have in the pot,' says he. We went, and the pot wasn't too far away. We came back to her with six dozen. He counted them one by one and handed three gold sovereigns to us. That was the catch of one day and one night. I told the captain so and that we had been up all night. We were pretty tired, but all the same our night was well paid. He told us at once to come on board. We begged his pardon, saying that we weren't far from home now. He wouldn't accept that, but made us come on board. 'We've got a meal ready here, and eat your fill,' says he.

We had to accept his invitation. We made a good meal. I was rather shy, being so smudgy and dirty in a place like that, but the other chap never gave it a thought; all he wanted was to fill his belly; he'd left all the shyness and nervousness of his early days in foreign lands, and he told me, too, that if I'd been away from home a bit, I wouldn't have cared what sort of a place I got food to eat in.

When I came on deck the captain was strolling up and down, and he began to question us about the lobsters, and he asked whether there were more of them about the

Island. We told him how things were. In a while we left him and bade farewell. When we reached the harbour, some of the others were just leaving it, and another lot were still in bed.

When we had landed the canoe, Pats said:

'We'd better take a bottle of milk and a dozen eggs out to the ship. We shan't be long.'

I liked to hear him speak in this generous style; though often enough he said things that didn't please me. Off I went along the Island, and he stayed where he was until I came back with two dozen eggs and a bottle of milk. We went out again to the little ship. I handed up the bottle and the box of eggs. One of the crew caught hold of them at once and took them on board—for they've no way of getting eggs and milk while they are ploughing the sea. When the box came back, it was full to the brim—biscuits, tobacco, a joint of meat—and to top all, when I searched the box afterwards, what should I find there but half a pint of whisky. We rowed in and went home and went to bed till dinner-time—a new thing for us to do.

After our dinner we went out again and began to pull up the pots and set them in trim ready for twilight, for that's the time when the lobsters go into the pots most—they don't like the middle of the day; it's too bright. As the sun was sinking into the sea, we fell to pulling them up again, and they were well filled. We made out then that the night is the best time for catching them. And from that time on we used to spend every fine night out on the sea, so that we made first-rate catches, and nobody knew.

Far on in the autumn, one fine night that we were anchored with a lobster pot rope, we heard a singing, soft and long and sweet, in the deep middle of the night, to the northward of us on some rocks that lay about half a mile from us. My heart leapt in me, and I felt very odd.

'Do you hear it?' said I to the other man.

'I hear it well enough,' said he.

'Let's be off home,' said I.

'Yerra, you poor wretch, they're only seals,' said he.

'They can't be seals, for they have a human voice!'

'Yes, they are indeed, and anyone can tell that you've never heard one of them before. It's their way to carry on like a human being when some more of them come ashore to join the rest, and there's a crowd of them high and dry on those rocks to the west now.'

I partly believed him, and I knew that these people that travel to the lands across the sea don't worry themselves over anything, dead or alive. And at that thought I had to give in.

Before long I heard it again, long and soft and sweet, and it sounded to me like 'Eamonn Mágáine', just as it might come from human lips; and all I could do was to keep my feelings down. As for the other fellow, he tuned up a song himself. They were singing in the west and he in the east. I fancy he did it to put heart in me.

Well, we took a shift out of the pots, and there was a good dozen lobsters in them.

'Have you got a dozen?' says he.

'I have exactly, neither less nor more.'

'Isn't it the devil's own pity you didn't fly off home at the crooning of the seals. You'd be badly left in the countries across the sea.'

No doubt he was right enough as far as that went, though at other times he was often pretty far out. He went on till he came to anchor on the same rope again, and, to top all, this was in the place where the seals could be heard most clearly.

While we were settling down there wasn't a whistle or a cry from anything; but before long they raised their voices in chorus, so that they could be heard everywhere around.

'I wonder what sets them raving like this now and again,' said I to the other chap, 'while they keep quiet at other times.'

'Every time a seal comes to them from the sea, that's when they go on like this. Another has just come ashore, and they were asleep till that happened.'

By this time they were singing so that none ever heard at market or fair so many songs in concert together, and the sound of the one song weaving in and out of the other. I cleaned him out of all he had to say about the seals, for he had a great deal of knowledge of things, far more than I who had never left the corner of the hearth.

'Wait till the day dawns—and I fancy it's not far off now—and you'll see something: all the seals high and dry on those rocks to the west,' said he.

'But I've often seen one of them by himself ashore on a rock,' said I.

'That wouldn't be all you'd have seen of them if it had been a habit of yours to be abroad in the night. You'll pay no attention to them the next night you hear them, my lad.'

I understood him very well by the time he'd got through with this last sentence, hinting, as it were, that I shouldn't fail to be eager to come the very next night! In a little while he said that the dapple of day was beginning to show in the east and we had just as well be shifting the pots again.

'Wait till there is more light in the day, and then we shall have less trouble looking for them from place to place.'

The upshot of it all was that it was bright enough by the time we moved, and at that very moment the singers went completely crazy, every last one of them tuning up in chorus.

'It won't be long till those lads over there will be leaving the rocks,' says Pats.

Soon the full light of day was come and we could see the seals in crowds on the ridge of the rock, some of them with their heads in the air, another one snapping at his fellows on this side and on that, and, far above them all, a huge big chap lying without a stir on the rock. The other man said to me that this fellow was still asleep, and that, when he should wake, then the hurly-burly would begin. You would have thought to listen to him that he'd spent his life among them, he was so much better at explaining them than I was.

We stayed anchored to our pot till nearly every one of them had taken to the water, and they wasted that much of the morning's work for us. At last the big fellow woke up out of his slumber, and when he lifted his head you could hear the savage scream he let out of him ringing all round. He was the foreman of the whole gang, big and little. Before long he started down.

He was a bull, as huge a bull as was ever on dry land. He shoved his snout under the seal next to him and flung him into the air as high as a boat's mast, and he never stayed in his flight till he came down out in the sea. Then began the fight at the fair when the rest of them saw that. They hurried to the water at their best speed, and, if any seal went too slow, when this chap came up with him, he put his snout under him and lifted him into the sky ever and always till he'd got them into the water, the whole crowd that had been high and dry on the rock, and there were a lot of them.

The big fellow stayed a while after them on the rock to take breath and to see if he had the whole herd together. Then he, too, plunged into the sea, and the two of us agreed that the wave he raised where he struck the water would have sunk a small ship. All the time this hurly-burly was going on they made neither whistle nor cry, believe me.

We should have had all our pots lifted and safe well enough while this row was going on, and I expected that the other chap wouldn't wait so long, but he did: I fancy that the tricks they were playing gave him just as odd a feeling as they gave me. We pulled up the pots quickly enough after this, for they were easily seen since there wasn't much water above them. We had made a fair catch by morning, a good three dozen. I tell you that, even though our canoe was a little one, the catch was big. We spent the whole season like this every fine night. Not much goes into the pots by day or night when the sea is troubled. The lobster likes to have the sea calm and quiet when he peers about him.

One morning we were ready to come home and there was a little breath of wind blowing from the west, and when we started there were some spars of drift timber to be seen. We picked them up. There were some more to be got in other places. We soon had the canoe full, and some more were still floating on the tide. We had to turn in to Beginish and clear the boat and push out once more. The driftwood was coming in masses round a point where there was a swirl of tide. There were white planks, absolutely new, afloat. We had to untie a rope from a pot and bind together a dozen planks with it and tow them in our wake and row back to where we had the rest and land them. We took sixteen of them that turn, and hoped to get more while that tide was running. The only thing that was troubling me now was hunger. It was heavy work after a night out, and the toil of getting the planks together was great, but we were determined to carry on so long as there was a piece adrift. As for the Yank, he never felt tired or hungry.

I let him know that I was getting hungry, and high time, too. I wanted to see what he would say, making trial of him, as it were.

'Yerra, my lad! surely you remember the old saying, "Take the fish while you can get him", or do you think that there'll be driftwood to be got any time you like?' says Pats.

I had expected that that would be the answer I should get, for I knew that he was right and that stuff of this kind isn't going all the time. We never stopped so long as the tide that was collecting the driftwood for us held. Our hunger passed from us as the time for taking food went by. A man grows gradually weaker from that time on, and so it was with us.

Later on in the day we saw first one boat and then another, gathering the driftwood like ourselves on this side and on that. By this time the two of us had saved about three-score white planks with the little canoe in Beginish. The poor lout of a Yank worked hard that day. Often enough we'd be a long way from the shore by the time I had a dozen planks tied up, and it was he who'd land them without any help from me.

We were all right, but then what about our people at home—we had left home just after dinner the day before, and now it was dinner-time on the next day and we hadn't returned—all they could think was that we were lost.

Any canoes that were about the houses at this time—and few they were, for they were in the little islands busied about their pots—the few that were not, were in quest of the driftwood by this time. And so there wasn't an oar or a canoe in the creek to go to look for us.

When we were weary and worn and the tide had turned and the timber was growing scarce, we set our face homewards; and I tell you, dear reader, if there had been a puff of wind against us, we should never have made it.

The talk of the village was the quantity of timber that the two of us, with our little canoe, had collected in Beginish, and for many days after that we found planks and fragments and pieces of timber. We sold about half of the Beginish stuff there, and the other half we had to bring home with us, for not a bit of saved timber could ever be left without being stolen.

20. *The Troubles of Life*

IN the early part of the year after the salving of the driftwood—and I believe we made a dozen pounds out of it,
not to speak of any lobsters—we were doing very well, but,
'the horse doesn't always keep up its pace'.

At the time when the young birds come and are beginning to mature, the lads used to go after them. My eldest
boy and the King's son planned to go to a place where they
were likely to get a young gull—for one of those would
often live among the chickens in a house for a year and more.

The two went together after the nests to bring a pair or
so of the birds home with them. They were in a bad place,
and, as my boy was laying hold of the young gull, it flew
up and he fell down the cliff, out on the sea, God save the
hearers! He remained afloat on the surface for a long time
until a canoe going after lobsters came up and took him
aboard.

His grandfather (his mother's father) was in the canoe
that took him in. We had only one comfort—there was no
wound or blemish anywhere on his body, though it was
a steep fall from the cliff. We must endure it and be content! It was a great solace to me that he could be
brought ashore and not left to the mercy of the sea. This
was the first beginning, and an ill one it was, God help us!

This happened about the year 1890, just when the boy
was developing and beginning to lend a hand. Well, those
that pass cannot feed those that remain, and we, too, had
to put out our oars again and drive on.

That year did not prove as good as the year before; and we didn't take as many lobsters in the night either, because of it, for the weather was never settled, and there was a constant swell round the rocks—a thing that this kind of fish dislikes. But it happened this year, nevertheless, that fish for curing came well inshore, and the sea was full of them. They were pollock—a large, coarse fish, very troublesome to get in over the boat's gunwale; they were caught with the line, a bit of mackerel for a bait, and a big hook.

We went after them one day with trappings of this kind, and we were so eager to catch them that we had to leave the fishing ground early, for we had the little canoe full and the sea was rough and disturbed; and when we came to the creek, many a man marvelled at what our little canoe had brought us.

We spent part of the year engaged with the fish for curing until we had filled every vessel we had in the house, and by then we had got three hundred pollock salted. There was always a great demand for them among the country people about Christmas for the festival.

I brought fifteen pounds with me from Dingle for my pollock; many of my relations got a couple of them as well, and there were plenty left at home for my own use.

A while after that the daughter of Big Daly, the herd of Inishvickillaun, came home from America. That was the girl whom my uncle, Diarmid the rake, used to be matching with me in the days of my youth. She spent a few years across the water, but her health failed—as is the case with so many others. After her return she got no better, but fell into a decline, though she had come to the healthiest island in Ireland.

She died at last, there on the island, during the fishing season. There were fishermen from Iveragh with them in the island at that time, and, when the news of her death

came, everybody who could did his best to get to the rock
to be at the wake.

They were the best and the most hospitable people that
ever lived on a rock of the kind, and for that reason everybody tried to get to them in their time of trouble, and
there was a great concourse of people collected there that
night. Canoes were coming to the island until ten o'clock
at night, and a great number of others made the passage
to the west across the bay in the morning, for it was a
lovely day and the sea was fine and calm. It was the finest
day for a funeral I ever saw, and the hottest. The coffin
was put into the Iveragh boat, and there was a crew of
three good men in her. When they were ready, they turned
their backs to the rock and started to make haste east across
the bay. When the funeral reached the harbour of the
island, more canoes were waiting for us. We had still to go
three miles of sea or more. When I threw my eye over
them I thought I had never seen so many canoes together.
There were eighteen of them. I never saw, nor have I seen
to this day, so many boats in a sea funeral. Sixteen or
fourteen is the most I have seen since. May God be com-
forting to the souls of all those whom I must needs bring
back to memory; and may He give no ill place to any one
of them.

Though the man in the Inish had a houseful of children
then, there are only three of them in my neighbourhood
now; the rest of them are in America, scattered east and
west as with so many others.

The world went on like this from year to year, and I was
still living in my old hovel of a house. The thought came
to me to leave it and make a shift to build another little
shelter, and not to have the hens clucking over my head
any longer. Though often enough we found a nest of eggs
up there in a day of need, yet all the same the drip used to
come through often in their wake. A kind of house was

coming into use at that time which had a timber roof on it—felt, and strips, smeared with tar, over that. They were as slippery as a bottle, and when a hen wanted to go up after her fashion to lay eggs she would fall down again into the yard, and would never try it again.

When a thing once comes into a man's mind, I fancy it has a way of sticking there, and that was my case in this matter of a house. I knew that I shouldn't get any help towards it, only that I had a sort of convenience in my old house being there for me, so that I could take my time over it. I didn't move farther than the breadth of a street, for I had the stones all round me, and I realized that it's easy baking next the meal, and that it was a great thing for me that the materials were all about me. I set to work at once designing the house, and when I had settled its length and breadth I felt as though I should have a palace when I got it up—well roofed with timber and felt and tar. I kept on adding a bit to it when I got the chance, and piece by piece it soon began to have the look of a house; and before long the body of the house had risen, and all I had to do was to put together the two gables, and they were soon narrowing in, one row of stones after another.

Well, I never had an idle moment for a whole quarter, and then I had set the 'crow stone'—that is, the last stone placed on the summit of the gable. I'd finished the job without anybody handing me a stone or a bit of mortar!

It was in the depth of winter that I set about this business of the house: for I shouldn't have had any chance of doing it in the busy fishing season—the time when I placed the last stone, as I've just said. Work was beginning about mid-March: there was the land to dig, and the weed for manure to fetch in the boats or from the beaches, and that was the time when people used to visit the seal caves.

One of those mornings—a fine, soft, lovely morning—there was a knock on my door before day-break, and, as I was only sleeping lightly, I sprang up at a bound and opened the door, and who should be outside but Diarmid.

'Dress yourself,' said he. 'The day is calm. We'll go west to the islands. Who knows what may be lying in a seal cave or in a creek? Have you a bite of bread cooked?'

'I've got bread enough,' said I, 'only I had no idea of going back to the islands. I fancy it would be a wasted journey so early in the year.'

'Yerra, we'll get something—a string of rabbits, or, perhaps, something better than that. How do you know we mightn't meet with a fine young seal? Take a good hunk of bread that'll do for the two of us.'

'Yerra, what an idle lump of a wife you've got!' said I to him. 'I suppose she's saving meal.'

'Devil a bit! only she's too lazy and doesn't care who's hungry,' says he. 'She's a fine, easy woman, and she never had much sense.'

I put up a good slice of bread, and we went our way together out of the door. The rest of the crew had come. We launched the boat on the water, and off we went. We never stopped till we got to Inish na Bró, where there was a famous seal cave. It was a very rare thing not to find a seal there. We said to one another that we had best search it.

In a moment there were four of us in the cave, for we were keen to leave the boat. We were moving up the cave, and one of the men started peering into a pool there.

'I wonder what those things in the bottom of this pool are?' says he.

One man after another took a look, and we saw that the hole was full of them.

One of the men in the boat was a great swimmer, and he came and looked down.

'Yerra, you devils!' said he, 'they're bolts of copper and brass. Don't you know that a hulk of a ship was wrecked here a bit ago and it was full of bolts of this kind?'

No sooner had he finished that much talk than he cast off every stitch of clothes and plunged his head under the water.

There was little more than a man's depth in the pool, and he hadn't been under long when he came to the surface again with a bolt of copper four feet long.

'By your shining soul!' says he, 'are you depending on me to bring up all that's here? Put a rope round one or two others, and you'd better look sharp before the tide comes, for it's hard to see them when there's any disturbance in the hole.'

That was what should be done; but where were the two to go under water? That was the problem. There were some of them who'd never been in the sea, and others of us who could swim well enough, but we hadn't the habit of going under.

Diarmid rushed across the beach to me. 'Aren't you a marvellous swimmer at other times, and often enough without anything to show for it?' said he. 'Come over here to me and loop this rope round you and fetch up one of those golden hurleys for us. Don't let's have to depend on one only, or on two for that matter.'

Well, even though I didn't like the look of things much, I didn't want to bring that lunatic on top of me, and so I did what he said. I threw off my duds and in I went to the bottom of the pool. The rake was very upset when he saw that I hadn't put the rope round me, as he had said. He thought that I was in a bit of a rage. But it wasn't so, for I stood in no need of a rope at all. All I had to do was to thrust myself to the surface when I wanted, for I was a good swimmer.

When I went down I hit upon a bolt with my foot, and I looked about me to see if I could find another one so that the rake would be surprised when he saw me coming with two of them, for the other chap only brought them up one at a time, and very set up with himself he was at getting that much.

Well, I searched about a lot, and before long I saw the second one and shifted it easily. One of them was under my oxter and the other in one hand, while the other hand was working for me. I put my feet in position and shot up lightly to the surface, but, even so, the weight of the bolts was dragging me down again, for it chanced that I had come to the surface in the very middle of the pool. But the rake played his part well. He flung the rope, and I caught it in my unemployed hand. When Diarmid saw me coming with the two bolts, then he began lilting. And he had no pity for me since I'd come through alive with something in my hands, for he was a man always keen on making a catch.

'Good for you! You may be slow, but you come heavy laden,' says he to me. 'Down with you again.'

Another man was standing on the brink of the pool. Maurice Bán they used to call him. He was a broad, strong man, and he'd never swum a stroke. He didn't like to see us going into the pool while he was looking on. He said to Diarmid:

'Tie the end of the rope to my body and I'll go down and bring an armful of those up with me, since there's such a lot of them.'

'Yerra, your soul to the swarthy devil!' says Diarmid, 'you must be going out of your senses. One might as well send a bag of salt down as you. Even the swimmers have nothing but the breath left in them when they come up!'

Maurice turned to the other man to tie the rope round him, when he saw Diarmid snarling at him; and that man was a brother of Diarmid's named Liam, who didn't give a curse whether Maurice came out of the hole dead or alive.

Liam tied the rope round Maurice, and down he went, and when he struck the bottom all he did was to pull at the rope again until he came to the surface without waiting for Liam to pull it up. It was well he did so, for Liam would have given him plenty of time to drown down there.

Before the water began to flood the hole the pair of us had twenty-one bolts, a fine heap of them, both of brass and copper; and it's long before Diarmid would have tired of dragging them out to the boat.

When we had everything ship-shape we began to chew our bread and gulp it down—we hadn't much to say till that was done—with nothing in the world to eat with it for sauce, only now and again a man would stretch out his hand and scoop up a handful of the salt water and send it down to clear his throat.

While we were fiddling about like this, just ready to start for home, Liam gave a look and saw a trawler making for Inishvickillaun.

'Something's bringing them to that place to-day,' said Diarmid.

When she came near the strand of the Inish she let go her anchor as though she meant to make a stay there.

'Well,' says Diarmid, 'out with your oars and let's see what has brought her, and then we'll be off home in God's name.'

We made our way across, for the two rocks are close to one another, and before long we were with them. She was full of people. The chief part of their business was to have a day's fun on the islands.

We had the bolts hidden in the boat so that nobody could see them, but in the end we said to one another that it would be a good idea to show them one of them to see what they would have to say about it. When a gentleman on board saw the brass spar, he wondered where we had come upon it, and asked us at once how much we wanted for it. It was a very long time before he got any answer, for nobody in the boat had any proper notion of it. At last the captain of the vessel spoke and said:

'This is a man who buys this kind of thing, and he would like you to sell it to him.'

Then we made out that he would buy all we had of them. In the end, to make a long story short, we sold the whole lot to him for sixteen pounds.

We had to go on board the trawler and take food and drink in her—and there was plenty of it to be had, and methinks the place to find plenty and to spare is where the gentry are. At last we said farewell to them.

As we were coming up to the other rock—that is, Inish na Bró—rabbits could be seen dancing on every blade of grass in it. They had the hot weather and the sun and pleasantness on the island to make them do it.

Suddenly, when we were just under the rock, Diarmid spoke. He was our captain. He jumped up now and said: 'It's a lovely, quiet evening, and we haven't a thing to do but go home. We've two good dogs in the boat and a couple of stout spades. Let's pay a visit to the rock and we'll have half a dozen rabbits apiece.'

For one man that fancied what he had to say there were two that didn't, but, all the same, every one of them liked hunting. The boat stopped at the landing-place, and out we went—two of us east and the other two west. It was late in the evening before we met one another again on the edge of the landing-place. The rake Diarmid wasn't the worst off for game. He had as much as any other two, only he had a fine dog of his own; besides, there wasn't a weak place in him or in the dog.

When we had all come to the boat and put the game together, we had eight dozen rabbits—a dozen apiece. The oldest men in the boat said that it was the best sport they ever remembered in the islands in so short a time. There was a smell of wind blowing fair for home.

As few people can keep a secret, it got abroad, from one of us, too, where we had spent the day, and what we had found, and all about the gentry who bought the brass: and, since the secret had got out, we had seen our last of the metals. Before we got together on the morrow the boats of the village were gone. But not many pounds were made out of it ever after. The two pounds I got from this were the first two pounds I paid for the roofing of the new house. Goods were cheap in those days, and the things I wanted for the new house didn't cost me very much. I had by me a lot of the things I needed for it, and it was a little house, although when I was designing it I fancied it was a palace; anyhow it was like a palace compared with the hovel I had. The hovel had one good point—that it gave me time to finish the new house without neglecting any of my other work; and there was another thing, too— there wasn't a thing in it that I had to transfer to the new house. I was at it from day to day, and from time to time, till I'd made a complete job of it. When I'd finished it, who should come by but Diarmid. He stopped to look for a bit, and then he said:

'Mary Mother! how did you put it together so quickly without help from a living soul? Wisha! blessing on your arms! My soul from the devil! but no hen will ever lay an egg on its roof, or, if she does go up, over the cliff she'll go!'

The house stayed like that, all built ready, some time before we went into it. There weren't many of the felt-roofed houses in the Island in those days, and now there hasn't been a house there for a long time without its covering of felt—all except those that are slated. We went to live in the new house about the year 1893, at the beginning of spring. Our chief reason for moving in so early was that manure was scarce that year, and there was as much manure in the old house as would have done for half the potatoes in the Island: there was nothing in it but soot and manure. Besides, Diarmid was worrying me every day. All he had planted were in very bad trim, for he was a poor fellow, all alone, and he'd calls to attend to everywhere. Too many calls often mean that things are clumsily done, and most of them show little profit. I used to be sorry for him, since the first wife he had was dead, and she had been a good one, while the wife he got next was neither handy nor tidy. Another reason I had for being fond of him —he would give us the very marrow of his bones when his help was needed.

So soon as Diarmid saw the fire and its smoke in the new house, in he came to me and put in a claim for the soot.

'For God's bright sake, don't let anybody else but me have it,' says he.

He was very keen on the look-out for something, but he would have been just as keen to give it away if he had it.

'I won't give your share of it to anybody else, have no fear,' says I to him. 'Have you got much to do to-day?'

'Holy Mary! wisha,' says he, standing between the two door jambs, 'I've nothing much on hand. Why do you ask? Do you need me at all?'

'Well, up you go on the roof of the old house and be clearing the manure for yourself.'

Up he went with a good will.

We had been some time in the new house, getting on very well, and thoroughly comfortable in it. A fine, clean house, without dust or smoke it was. We hadn't been living long in it when whooping-cough, and measles with it, came our way. Three months I spent sitting up with those of my children who took them worst, and I got nothing for the time I spent, only the two best of them were carried off. That was another discouragement for us, God

GATHERING FURZE ON THE HILL

GOING UP THE HILL FOR TURF

help us, and be sure that trouble went against us for a long time. However things went with me, I fancy the sorrow of it never left the mother for good or ill, and from that time forth she began to fail, for she was not to live long, and never lasted to be old.

Well, after all this anguish, I was trying to pull myself together. It was imprinted on my mind that there was no cure for these things but to meet them with endurance as best I could, and I kept trying to get through a while more of life—one year good and two that turned out ill.

A few years later a lady from the capital of Ireland came to this Island on her holidays. Eileen Nicholls was her name; and she hadn't been here long when she made a friend of a girl, and the one she chose was a daughter of mine. The two of them spent a part of every day together. One day they would be on the hill, another about the strand and the sea; and when the weather was soft and warm they used to go swimming. One day, when they were bathing, a strong spring tide was running, and when they thought it time to swim in to land they found themselves drifting away from it until they were exhausted. It chanced that one of my sons was digging potatoes in the garden near the house—this was in the beginning of harvest—a vigorous lad, and a good swimmer. He was eighteen years old. He saw the two girls swimming, and saw who they were at once, and that they wouldn't be able to get ashore.

He threw his spade away and took the shortest cuts down the cliff and the beach until he came to the strand. He didn't take off a thing, his boots or anything else, for they weren't too far out, and when he came down to the water he saw the lady sinking. Out he went and spoke to his sister. He told her to keep herself afloat on the surface for a while; that as the lady was drowning, he would go to her assistance first. He went, and he and the lady were drowned together. Another man brought in the sister, who was at her last breath. The boats took up the other two just as Pats and I were returning as usual from our fishing. That was the sight that awaited us.

Well, I had to face this trouble, too, and go through it. It was the biggest funeral Dunquin had ever known. They were carried together until they parted, going, each one of them, to their family burying place. The lady's family were very kind to me for years afterwards. They both came, the father and the mother, to see me in Dunquin and had me pointed out to them. I hope they did not think that I was angry with them because my son had died for their daughter. I was never so foolish as that. If it was for her he died, it could not be helped. It was God's will.

I think that if it hadn't been for my uncle Diarmid, I should never have recovered from this trouble at all. I had God's help, too, for the daughter who had been in the sea was never expected at first to come round either, since she was still at her last breath. I felt that, if I could be assured that even she would recover, things would not be so bad with me. Diarmid used to come in every day and night, making little of our despondent talk, reminding us of troubles far worse than ours—a ship lost at sea with hundreds on board; a wall of rock falling on all the workers in a mine—so as to put heart in us.

His own good fortune didn't last long. He had some fine strapping lads at this time, and before long he would have been able to do what he pleased if things had gone well with them, with no trouble in the world but to issue orders to them. A little while after my trouble he came in to me and I suspected nothing.

'Something's brought you now,' said I to him.

'Misfortune has brought me,' said he.

'What is it?' said I to him, for I was impatient for him to speak.

'It is this,' said he: 'late last evening the best of my lads was running after a sheep and he stumbled as he ran, and fell, too, and a sharp rock hit him on the brow, and he lost a great deal of blood. It isn't so much the size of the cut, but there is a deep hole in his head, and I fancy that a piece of the bone inside is broken.'

'And what are you to do now?' I said.

'I want the priest and the doctor,' said he. 'As the day is fine, get yourself ready.'

'I'll be with you in a minute,' said I to him. 'Get the rest of the crew.'

When we got to Dunquin, two had to go for the priest and two others took the road to Dingle. Diarmid himself and his brother Liam went that way. I and Pats Heamish went for the priest. They had ten miles to go, and I promise you they had to go and return on foot, without a horse or a foal.

When we reached the priests' house they were out, and we had to wait quietly until they returned; we spent a lot of the day there. The parish priest asked us if the case was dangerous, and we said it was. It was settled that the young priest should come with us. We started off before him, and we took all there was in them out of our legs, for we knew that the priest would be before us, do the best we could, though we were taking a short cut.

When we reached the harbour at Dunquin, the doctor hadn't come yet. The whole day was gone by this. The priest wasn't kept long, however. We launched the boat, and we were just starting when the other two appeared on the crest of the cliff, and the doctor with them. We turned back and took them on board. It was black night by the time we reached the Island. To be sure, we had to go out once more and come back again.

They saw that the boy was in danger, and the doctor said that, if any fragment of the bone inside was broken, it would always be troubling him. 'But,' said he, 'he'll be all right if that isn't the case.'

That was no idle day for us, and that's how it always is in an island like this—grinding toil always when the time of trouble comes.

The lad never did a profitable day's work from that till he went to the churchyard.

21. *The Yellow Meal*

THE CAPTAIN OF THE DINGLE SMACK · THE MEAL
PUT ABOARD · THE COASTGUARD · A DIFFICULT
PASSAGE TO THE ISLAND · BUYING THE BONHAMS

THAT year was a hungry year in the Island, and in many
other places, too, and a gentleman set out from the capital
of Ireland to find out where the scarcity was, and he came
as far as the Blasket. He sent an order for meal and flour to
Dingle. We went there to fetch it.

There was an old trawler in the harbour, and she hadn't
done a stroke of work for a long while. There was a man's
length of seaweed growing on her—winkles, limpets, and
mussels. The old captain who had command of her was like
to be in the same case as his ship. The bristle of hair that
sprouted out of him when he was young was on him still,
undisturbed, flowing down to his breast. And you wouldn't
believe that a single drop of water had touched him since
the days of the great famine. He wasn't a single day less
than eighty. Some good man in Dingle advised him to earn
the pence for himself and for his crazy old galley that had
never shifted from the slime of the harbour for five years
past.

She was brought up level with the quay. Soon the last
load was aboard her. Then a coastguard came along the
quay and fell to talking with the captain. He asked where
was the rest of the ship's crew. The old lad said that he
didn't need much of a crew—two besides himself.

The King's man was a strong, vigorous fellow, and he
was by way of being angry with him.

'It isn't you we ought to blame,' says he, 'but the people
that had anything to do with you, you and your devil's
carrion of a ship; and I wouldn't wager half a crown on its

chance of making the Island. Have a crew ready by the time I come back, for, if you haven't, I'll take out of her everything that's in her and put it in another boat.'

The reason why the King's man spoke so shortly to him was that he had been intending to go along with him. The white-haired ancient nearly spurted blood from his nose. He turned blue instead of grey. He rushed the whole length of the quay after the other man, but the Islanders kept him off. When they stopped him, he shouted out like a mad bull:

'By the devil's pulleys, you go on as if you had the right to my boat. And who gave it you?' says he to the coastguard.

'Is there a man of you there from the Island who could raise the sails to the masthead for me and go with me?' says he, with a wild look in his eyes.

Though the Islanders were in sore need of the meal and flour, they were none too ready to answer him. One of them said they had no notion of the job. He'd just said that much when the King's man came at a trot down the quay with a bundle in his hand as though he had his day's provision put together. The white-haired man didn't spot him till he had jumped aboard.

'Have you got any hands since?' says he.

'What the hell is it to you whether I have them or not?' says the ancient mariner.

Just then there were two peelers standing on the quay. The coastguard ordered them to take the old fellow in charge. He'd ruined the alms of the poor, for the water was already leaking on to the meal, and there was no one in charge of the old hulk to pump her or bail her. The pair gripped the old man.

The King's man asked our King if he would shirk going aboard the old smack with him and some other good fellow in his company. The King agreed, as was his way when there was need of him—for he was both King and mariner when the call came, as well as being just as handy at planting potatoes and carrying manure for them; many a time has he harnessed his old, grey, bobtailed ass when all else in the place were in their slumbers. He got another man to go with him.

The King came to me before they put to sea. He showed me a box, and put it in my charge. They went aboard, and the man there set them their tasks at once, and before long the old tub was ready to start from the quay. Then the King's man shouted to the peelers, asking if the old captain was agreeable to go with them now, though he wouldn't have any authority over the ship.

Though the white-haired man wasn't too well pleased, he knew very well that, if he wasn't on the ship, he wouldn't get any pay. So he went aboard. The King's man called on another Dingle lad so that he might be with them on their journey home. Then off they started.

The rest of us started off to trudge the way home. We had a lot of trifles with us, and we couldn't carry them on our backs, so we needed a cart. We got it for seven shillings. We threw our stuff into the cart, and I put in the King's box very carefully, and never took my eyes off it till we reached Dunquin. There were bottles in it, and nobody was to be trusted in their neighbourhood. The King's box had rounded Slea Head when he was no farther than the mouth of the Dingle Harbour, for we could see them there.

There wasn't any wind to move the ship, even if she had been any good, but when we had just reached the cliff above Dunquin Harbour a stiff breeze began to blow. We hurried up for fear that the old captain would make the Island before us, since he'd got the wind; but we needn't have hurried. When we came to the Island there was no sign of the ship. As the night drew on, people went up on the hill to see if they could get a sight of her in the bay, and there was a lump of something that looked like her tacking from side to side just off Ventry Harbour.

One man from every house in the Island stayed up all night. When the morning light came, the old hulk was to be seen off Slea Head without a stitch of canvas on her except a piece on each mast about half the size of a woman's shawl.

Well, it mattered little how she looked since they'd come through by giving her her head and letting her drive on. One after another the men went to their food this way and that, to pass the time till she came to harbour.

But, as the morning went on, she never came an inch nearer. Before long some of the men went down to the creek brink and decided to go out to her with a boat or two, and so they launched a canoe and a little boat, for there were no big boats then, nor had there been for some time past. When we got to the ship, there wasn't a man on board that looked like himself after the night, even the King. It seemed that they had spent the night pumping water out of the old trawler, and she needed it still. They'd had to strike the mainsail for fear the old boat would split and go down under their feet. It's a stiff job pumping a ship.

We tied two ropes to her, and, as the tide was with us, before long we'd brought her to her anchorage. There were eight tons of both meal and flour in her, a great help to the Blasket at that time. When we fell to carrying it home, you'd have thought the harbour was an ant-hill, for every man had his bag on his back. When the two Islanders left the old tub, the only crew left aboard were the three others; we got the anchor aboard for them.

The King didn't forget to ask after the box he'd entrusted to me when he went on the ship; and when I told him that it was waiting for him at home, safe and sound, he was mighty pleased, and forgot all the troubles of the night.

Well, if the Blasket houses had lacked food earlier on in the year, they couldn't say that now since the old tub had managed to make a job of it. It's an old saying that God's help is nearer than the door, and that's no lie; all that lashings and leavings of food had come when we least expected it. The next thought that entered our minds was that it would go mouldy before half of it could be consumed, and that we had best find a way of getting some good out of it while it was sound. The plan we pitched on was to go and buy some bonhams and, when the last of the meal was finished, to begin grumbling again.

We'd only been an hour settling on this scheme when every man had shaved and put on clean duds, and every canoe in the Island was at sea making for Dunquin. When we got to the harbour on the mainland, the whole parish was gathered waiting for us. They thought that it was a funeral on the way, and it seemed odd to them that they hadn't heard tell of anybody's death.

A relation of mine came over to me across the beach.

'Yerra, my heart!' says he, 'you must have come on some important business since all the canoes have come out together.'

'It's a great wonder you didn't manage to ask somebody else about that before you came to me,' says I.

'Yerra, my heart! some of them are not above telling you a lie. They've got a bit of the playboy in them, and I'd find it hard to believe what most of them would say.'

'We're going to buy bonhams,' says I.

'Holy Mary! and me thinking that the most of them there hadn't a bite to put in their mouths. And isn't it a strange thing for you to be going to buy the makings of pigs without a penny to do it with?' says he.

His words maddened me, for he was a mean fellow himself, whose ways were not to my taste.

'If that's a tale you've heard, the man that heard it

isn't up to much, though there are many of your kin in the Island. And it seems that you hadn't much feeling for them when you heard that report, since you had a score or so of bites of food yourself and never visited them to give them a single one of those bites.'

'You're a bit out of temper, and that isn't often the way with you,' says he, and sheered off.

When we had landed the canoes, we made our way to Dingle on foot, ten miles. The country folk were startled when they saw every man of us buying two or three bonhams.

'Yerra, my heart!' said an old woman who'd sold us bonhams, 'sure it's a long way you are yet from the early potatoes to be buying bonhams, and yet what a lot of them they've bought to-day. And I have heard that some of the Islanders haven't a bite to eat themselves, and where have they got help from?'

'Och! it's little you know of the way of the world, or don't you know that He who puts us on short commons at one time gives us plenty at another time.'

We told her the whole tale.

'Holy Mary! it's long before other people would be helped like that,' says she.

'But didn't you get it before we did?' says one of us.

'How so?' says she.

'Because God gave you plenty of your own and left us with little,' and at that he left the countrywoman.

Forty-two bonhams came to the Blasket at that push. I had two of them, and I give you my word I had enough to do with them, and any man that had three would rather that the third one had been drowned in the end: for from the very day we bought the bonhams the alms failed. It was said that an ill report of us had got about. Anyhow my two bonhams did splendidly, and I hadn't had them on my hands long when I got nine pounds for them.

Any time we had pigs for market we had to spend two or three days in Dingle with them, and, often enough, a week in the depth of winter. I and my two pigs spent three nights and three days in Dingle that bout, till I'd spent half the money I got for them—and that's the reason why we've given them up entirely for more than twenty years now.

22. *The Wake*

THERE used to be a market every Saturday in the town in those days, and I had only just got rid of the pigs, got the money for them, and was thinking of setting out for home without delay, when I saw a Dunquin man coming my way down the street with a horse and cart, the horse foaming and sweating plenty.

As soon as I saw him stop and start to unyoke the horse, I went towards him to see what he had to tell. He told me that he was fetching stuff for his mother's wake, for she was in the next world since midday. A woman of the village was with him: that is one of the old customs from generation to generation. The dead woman was close kin to me, and so I, of course, gave up any thought I had of making the Western Island or going home.

The man who had come for the goods for the wake told me that another cart had come in with him, and that, if I cared to stay with them, I could have a lift on that cart; there would only be a barrel of porter, and a trifle besides in it. I stayed by them, for I must be at the funeral on the morrow somehow. We had a drink or two—we two and the man who was going to give me a lift. The other chap went off to see if the coffin was ready, for that was what was holding them back now. It was then that I asked the other man about the porter, and asked was it that they were going to have both a wedding and a wake!

'Yerra, my friend, no! don't you know that barrel's for the wake?'

'But I've never heard of such a thing at a wake nor ever seen it before this,' says I.

'O! it's been coming into fashion for some time now, and, since it is so, no doubt he'll have a barrel, too.'

Soon the two came back to us, and the coffin was ready. Then we turned west. We didn't go very fast, for there were brittle things in the carts, and so it was night by the time we got to the house in Dunquin, where the body was. There was a good share of people gathered there by this, and the night was beginning to fall. All our things were taken indoors. We unyoked the horse. A lamp was burning in the house and a candle or two. Two women jumped up and laid hold of the candles and arranged them properly at the end of the table.

I sat myself down near the door when I went in, but I wasn't left there long. The man of the house found me out and waved his hand to an empty chair in the corner, and told me to stick to it till somebody else should take it from me. I was well pleased with the man of the house for looking after my comfort in this way, for I had been away from my house and my home village for days, and I was pretty well worn out. Besides, it was no dark corner where the chair happened to be, and, what I liked even better than that, I could see all over the house and notice everything.

The feet of the corpse were to the fire and its head to the door. On the other side, facing the door, was the whole set-out. I hadn't been in the corner long when the house began to fill. There was a great flame of fire, a kettle on the hook above it, two kettles at the side of it, and the gathering was beginning—men, women, and children up and down throughout the house. At this moment four people were arranging the corpse finely. 'A dress for the journey to the other side', as one of the women said when they had it done.

Soon after they had sat down, four young women jumped

up and laid down a door lid across two stools, and before long I saw all the crockery in the house put together and arranged on the door. Soon I saw two pots for tea coming to the edge of the ashes, two women carrying one, and one the other. They put tea into them and filled them up with boiling water till the two were full to the brim. The other two women were bringing white bread till the door lid was covered all over.

As I was casting an eye over all these preparations, I saw a man coming up towards me from the bottom of the house with a great white bucket running over with porter in one of his hands, and an empty mug to hold about a pint in the other. The first man who met him after he'd come through the door, he shoved the mug down in the bucket and filled it and handed it to him. He didn't say: 'Take it away.'

Well, I knew in my corner that the whole pint wouldn't be long going down his gullet, for I knew the man who had it in his hand well—a man that'd drink the stuffing out of the saddle, and you could see the signs of his habits on him. I kept my eyes fixed from my corner on those who were handing out the food and drink, and I never saw anyone give the back of his hand to the bucket or the stuff in it till it came to where I was. I turned it down, and the man who was sharing it out was startled. It isn't that I like to break a custom—I've never done it—but I didn't care for the drink that was going round, for I've hardly so much as tasted it ever.

Just then the man who could read my disposition right— the man of the house, I mean—was at the other man's heels with a bottle of whisky and a glass, and he said to him:

'Don't you know he's no porter drinker?' He filled me up a glass out of that bottle and I drank it.

I glanced over to where the candles were flaming at the

end of the table, where were the feet of the corpse, and there were two men there, seated on chairs, who were busied over tobacco and pipes; and that was no pleasant job. One of them was cutting it and bruising it, while the other man was crumbling it small and stuffing it into the pipes; and if I didn't feel much more pity than jealousy of those two, I certainly didn't feel less, for often enough before I'd seen a good man faint at that job.

I hadn't been thinking so long when one of them tumbled down from the chair and fell right on the flat of his back on top of two bouncing women who were sitting on the floor with more than enough to do already. And the job these two women were at was trying to get a good blast of smoke out of two blunderbusses of pipes crammed with fresh tobacco, and all they had to do it with was matches; and it would take a machine a day to make all the matches they had wasted on the job, and the pipes were still unlighted.

When the man fell on the women, they didn't bless him very heartily, for the stems of the two pipes cracked and splintered in their mouths just when they'd got them ready with a lot of trouble, and it only wanted one more match to crown all their labours!

When this man that fell had been lifted to his feet—and he doesn't deserve to be called a man, but a wretch, for if a decent man had been at his job, he'd have left it sooner; but he was trying to make himself out a man, a thing not in his power the day tobacco got the better of him—he was like a man in a swoon. One said that a drop of water should be thrown over him, another that he ought to be given a taste of whisky, but I said they should give him plenty of tobacco, maybe that's what he wanted!

I hadn't felt any liking for him from the moment that I first noticed him fiddling with the tobacco; and I knew that nobody had put the job on him, only his own interferingness; and I told the man of the house to chuck him down the room, that he wouldn't get his death of it. They lifted my rascal out of the place where he was, and he'd only been cleared out when I heard one of the women saying this to him:

'May the next pipes and tobacco be at your own wake!'

As she said it, she gave a glance at the other woman by her and nudged her, but the second woman neither waked nor stirred.

'Devil take you, how soon you've collapsed!' says she, shaking her harder; but it was the same story. One woman after another came where she was. Someone brought a cup of spring water. They poured a drop over her out of a spoon, and they saw her coming to herself bit by bit.

I had a fine view of them, as I've said before, from the corner where I was placed; and, another thing, I was glad to have that view, for this was the first wake out of the Island that I was ever at.

There was a man sitting by me all the time, a fine, well-spoken man, smoking away at his fine white gun of a pipe.

'I wonder what happened to the man who was stuffing tobacco into the pipes,' says he to me, 'the man that was overset and that I haven't seen since?'

'It was his own insufficiency that did for him first, for he wasn't capable of doing a job like that. Besides, he'd drunk a pint bottle of whisky with the two women opposite that he fell on top of, and one of them fainted after him.'

'And what a sticker the woman there must be, if she had a man's share of the bottle,' says I to him.

'She's the one that got the bottle from the man of the house to share it between the three of them, and I expect half of it is in her stomach.'

'And how disobliging they were to you though you were on the spot!' says I.

'It's fifteen years since as much as a drop of it went into my body. The devil carry it from me!' said he.

I had seen the door in the middle of the kitchen all this time, but by the time they had these casualties cleared tidily away (whatever hole they shoved them in for quiet) the tea was going. There was everything there in plenty and profusion and leave to draw on it—white bread, jam, and tea; there was no butter there, and there never is in houses of this kind. I wasn't the last man to be invited to the board, for the man of the house came to me quickly, and took me and my chair with him, and put me where I could get something, saying:

'You're not like the rest. They're beside their own home, but you are some way from yours.'

I ate my fair share of it, but I didn't overdo it, for I didn't want to make a show of myself in a place of this kind, with a man from the east and a woman from the west present; and, if I was cradled in an island in the midst of the great sea, nobody ever had to complain of my awkwardness or ill manners. A new lot would come to the table when one lot was done until all the company were satisfied, and they'd chat a little till the bucket would come round now and again.

So we spent a good part of the night; tobacco going in plenty; some of them sending their pipes three times to the tobacco place to be refilled; and all that before the day lightened. About two o'clock the man next me pointed his finger across to the other side of the house where there was straw on the floor, and what should I see there but all the women in the house nodding with sleep now that all their fiddle-faddle of work was done.

At the dawn of day there was another meal going, but the people whose houses were near didn't take it. About midday or one o'clock all the people were gathered for the funeral, and when the priest came they started off towards the churchyard. But the journey wasn't far. Her family burying place was in Dunquin.

That was the wake that interested me most, and the reason was that there was drink at it—a thing I had never seen before. There have not been many wakes since without a cask or two, and I don't think much of the practice, for it's the usual thing that wherever there is drink there is horseplay, and that's not a fit thing in a house of the kind.

The funeral was on a Sunday, and all the Islanders who were ashore went to it, and it was late in the evening before we got home. I've often heard the old people say that a visit to the town did them more harm than a week's work at home—and that was true, but this time we were a week away because we had the pigs, though one of us used to say that he could live there for ever.

Well, that was the end of the pigs fed on the charity meal and of all the bonhams that were bought in one day at the Dingle market.

'Anyone might have known that no luck or good fortune would follow them,' said the poet to me one day.

'I'm sure you will give a reason for what you say,' said I.

'I'm the man for it!' says he. 'When this meal came and was landed below the houses, and then all the bonhams in Dingle market were bought to eat it, that was a strange thing,' said the poet.

'But you haven't produced an explanation of what you said just now,' says I.

'No, only half of it. Haven't you ever heard that there are two sides to a story? When the meal and those bonhams came to this island, it was the talk of all Kerry. There wasn't a man on a hill or on a strand, or a woman in a street or at chapel who chattered about anything else but the meal and the bonhams of the Island, and neither luck nor good fortune ever attended anything that runs in people's talk.'

'It's likely that there'll never be a pig or a bonham here again,' said I to him.

'That's the idea I have,' says he.

His idea was correct, for there's never been a pig or a bonham in the Island since. If the young people of the Island saw a pig or a bonham in the place, they'd go out of their senses.

Since I'm talking of the poet, I may as well have something to say of him here. It is about thirty-three years since Shane Dunlevy died. It was in the Island he died, after being ill for some time. He had had enough of his life in this world. As he said himself:

> '*Of all miseries told 'tis the worst to grow old,*
> *With no man to heed or respect you.*'

The poet had a great character when he was young. It's often I heard my mother talking of him. She was alive in his day. He had great stuff and spirit in him—he'd leap every dyke as he went to Mass of a Sunday; and he was always to be remarked among the men near him for his carriage and his character. I knew his character better than anybody else though he was old in my day. I fancy that his first nest—that is to say, his cradle—was in Ballinaráha in Dunquin. He married into the Island, a woman of the Manning family, a marvellous woman. She it was who finished the bailiffs and the drivers who used to come here day after day ruining the poor, who had nothing to live on but famine. A bailiff climbed on to the roof of her house and started knocking it down on her and on to her flock of feeble children. She seized a pair of new shears and opened them—one point this way, the other that. A stout woman and a mad woman! The bailiff never noticed anything till he felt the point of the shears stuck right into his behind. It wasn't the roof of the house that came in through the hole this time, but a spurt of his blood. That's the last bailiff we've seen.

Dunlevy was angry with the crowd that stole his sheep—and well they earned his anger—and he had to make a savage song[1] about them. He spent a part of his life in destitution, like many another. Nobody ever had the least thing against him; he was always a merry man. God's blessing be with them all!

I hadn't been long home when my uncle Diarmid met me, and he had a sorry story to tell me. His second son was failing, and he had got no sleep the night before.

'How came that?' said I.

'O, my dear, he was half out of his wits,' said he.

'But maybe it is that he's sickening for something,' said I.

'I don't know,' said he. 'But I'm afraid that his job's done.'

'Yerra, man, take it easy. How many things happen to people and they shake them off!'

Well, he spent a day or two more without coming into my sight.

'Surely,' said I to myself, 'it's not much out of my way to go where they are and see how things are with them, one with another, for he was always a good stand-by in the day of need.'

At that thought I sprang up, and never stopped going till I reached the house. The poor fellow was in a bad way. I asked him was his son getting better or worse.

'It's increasing on him,' said he.

I was sad and sorry for my poor old uncle, for he'd often come to me to quieten and steady me when I was in trouble; and I had rather that it had been the death sickness that had come upon his son, and so would he, too.

[1] 'The Blackfaced Sheep': a satirical poem against the neighbours who stole a sheep from him.

Death is a fine thing compared with some troubles that hang over a poor sinner.

I went out of the door and left the poor rake—and, though I've often given him that name in this book, it was a wrong name, for he was no rake, but just the opposite. But he was a hapless rake that morning, with all his troubles upon him.

On the morrow of that day my uncle was with me before I got to him. When I saw him, I knew well that he had no good news.

'I have no tale to tell, dear heart, but a tale of woe,' said he. 'The people tell me that if he could be in the hospital that would be the best place for him, where he'd have the doctor. But I fancy that we can't manage him easily in the canoe.'

To tell the truth, the job didn't please me too well. But what was to be done? Isn't the day of need the day when you have to stand to?

We went together—four of us—to see what we had best do, all of us pretty down in the mouth, particularly as we had to go on the sea on a job of this kind.

Well, when a thing has to be done, you may as well get yourself in trim to do it or give it up. We launched the best canoe we had, and then we went towards the house where the sick man was.

Things don't turn out as you expect often, and so it was in this case. You wouldn't have thought that there was a thing in the world troubling him all the time we were dressing him and otherwise making him ready. He went with us to the harbour as easily as he had ever done. Off we started. His father sat by him in the stern of the boat, and four of us were rowing hard to make the passage as short as possible till we reached the harbour at Dunquin. We came home again. The father came home next day, when he had settled the lad in the place that had been arranged for him.

He told me that the poor lad had never once played a trick on him all the way.

It was only a short time till I had to suffer more trouble, for, after all this had gone over me, my own wife died. I was completely upset and muddled after that, though she left two little girls to help me, but there is no great use in the like of them, and even if there had been, when comrades part, the one that remains can but blunder along only too often, and so it was with me. I had to turn my attention to everything, and, do what I would, things would often go wrong. My low spirits did not leave me soon this time, though I was always struggling to shake them off day by day, and, Heaven knows, I had but poor success in it. Something would always be coming across me to wake my trouble again.

The coming season was the time for taking mackerel. We would be abroad in the night and struggling to work by day. We were out one night, and it was a night to beat all others. It was beginning to look dirty, too, and we had to take shelter under the land. We hadn't been there long when another canoe came up to us with a load of fish in the nets—a proof that there was fish to be had if only the badness of the night had not prevented us from taking it. After a bit it looked to us as though a break had come in the bad weather, and we started out again, four canoes of us. When we got to the place where the other people had seen the fish, we cast out our nets, but the last mesh had only just left the canoe when there came violent rain and thunder and lightning so that you couldn't distinguish east from west.

I said to myself that we had best take in the nets again, and nobody contradicted me. I went to the stern of the canoe and ran and took hold of the rope. I dragged at it till I had the net, and two of us fell to pulling it aboard, one working at the corks and the other at the foot. Rarely had any pair to toil so hard as we, dragging the net on board in a gale of wind, with the sea breaking over us, and when we had the last of it in, there wasn't a glimpse of the world to be had anywhere for the rain and wind.

We got out the oars, and off we went working together, but we couldn't do a thing, because we had to keep our heads down, and we had to depend all the time for our guidance on the man in the bows. He had his head turned trying to keep his eye on the land, though in the end he could see no more than we could, but had to go by guess.

At length we got back to the place we had started from, and one of the canoes had got there first: this was the boat that told us they had seen the fish. She had cut away her nets so that they had only half of them on board now, but they didn't worry at all over the loss of the rest; they were only too thankful to have got away in safety. For some time we didn't know what had happened to the other two boats, but they, too, reached us in the end.

That was the first fright I ever had on the sea, but it wasn't the last. It doesn't matter if one or two feel frightened, for often enough some such would be terrified when the others didn't mind, but that night every man in the canoes admitted that that was the worst night they had ever struggled through.

Well, when we'd got to the creek the storm eased a little. We talked it over, and came to the conclusion that maybe the end of the night would be fine, and, since it was the way of the fish to swim on the surface, we should probably meet with a catch that would pay us for all our agony.

It was so. We acted accordingly, and left the canoes only just up from the water and hastened home all of us and ate some food in the middle of the night. The night was coming on splendidly. When I'd done eating, I went out to the landing-place, and they were coming out of the houses, man by man, going down to the boats. Some of the rest of the Island fishermen had been deep asleep from the beginning of the night.

Off went our four canoes again, and we never stopped till we'd reached that place in the sea where we had spied the fish in the storm earlier on. We paid out the nets, and they hadn't been out long when you could hear the clatter of fish as they went into the nets right to the very end. Any boat that hadn't her load from her own nets, got more than it could carry from another boat, and in the upshot we had to throw some of the fish into the sea, and some of the nets, too. The morning was coming on, and the four canoes came into the creek brimful with all the fish they could possibly carry. It was a lovely, calm morning, and our four boats started off for Dingle, taking the sea passage, for we could get an extra shilling a hundred there, and, since we could make that much more, we said that it would be to our advantage instead of taking it to Dunquin and paying for cartage.

We ran up the sails, and we had a good smell of wind with us—and that suited us very well, for our boats were down to the gunwale. We got to the quay in the end without wasting too much time, and one dealer bought everything in the four boats at fifteen shillings the hundred.

It's an old saying: 'The lazy lounger doesn't catch fish.' We had fish, for we were no loungers, but those that were got no fish, being asleep.

We had good purses of money now. There were over three thousand fish in each of our boats. We went to a house for food first, and after that to the tavern. We sang half a dozen songs, and that was no marvel, for if there were poor men of our kin, they weren't us that day. We had had enough to eat and to drink, and, more, there was a generous chink of money in our pockets.

Before we left the town we heard the news that the lad from the Island was in a good way, and we were to tell his father to fetch him; and, though it was late in the night by the time we reached home, I didn't go to bed without going with my good news to my old uncle, you may be sure.

The next day was Sunday, and I thought I should have to go on my journeys again with my uncle, since we couldn't fish that night, but he had thought for me and didn't bother me.

Well, the lad came back to the place he had left late that Sunday, and be sure the whole village went to meet him. There wasn't a thing in the world to notice or remark in him different from any other day, and everybody said that he was finished with his trouble.

That was nothing but guesswork, and sometimes people guess wrong. About three months after this people began to notice that he wasn't keeping steady in his wits, and his family kept an eye on him. One night when all in the house were asleep he slipped out and couldn't be found in the morning. Early that morning my poor uncle came to me, and it wasn't the look of a joker that he had. Everybody in the village went to look for him, but he wasn't to be found, dead or alive, God save us! and we had to throw in our hand.

The Island is three miles long by the old measurement, and the point farthest west from the houses is called the Black Head. Two men had gone there one day on some job or other—I fancy they were hunting—and they had dogs. The dogs left them and went under a big rock there, and, though the men whistled two or three times, the dogs didn't come. One of the men sprang down, and when he looked under the flagstone what should be there but the clothes and the boots of the missing man. An odd feeling came over them, and they hastened home, hunting no more that day.

When they got to the houses they didn't like to go and

tell the true story to the father, but one of the lads was a friend of mine, and they decided to come and tell me first and leave it to me to break the news to his family. It was nearly as bad for me as for them. Anyhow, when I came unexpectedly on poor Diarmid, I asked him to listen, and said:

'He's gone, and you have mourned him well already, and you may as well make the best of this piece of news of him.'

'I will,' said he.

I told him.

Three weeks after this his body was brought round by the great sea. A boat from the Island came upon him and saved it, and he is buried in Castle Point in the Great Blasket. The blessing of God's Grace on his soul!

23. *I begin to take an Interest in Irish*

SOME years before this it often happened that I would be held prisoner now and again out on the mainland in the winter season. In the house where I used to stay the children were always going to school. The Irish language was being taught in the Dunquin school in those days—as soon as it was in any school in Ireland, I think. The children of this house used to read tales to me all the time whenever I happened to be in their company until I got a taste for the business and made them give me the book, getting one of them by turns to explain to me the difficulties that occur in the language—marks of aspiration, marks of length, and marks of eclipse. It didn't take me long to get so far that I hadn't to depend on them to read out my tale for me once I understood the differences. For my head was full of it, and, if I came across a limping sentence, all I had to do was to hunt for it in my own brain. I could find the correct form of it without troubling anybody.

Very soon I had a book or two, and people in this island were coming to listen to me reading the old tales to them, and, though they themselves had a good lot of them, they lost their taste for telling them to one another when they compared them with the style the books put on them. It would be long before I tired of reading them to them, for I was red-hot to go ahead.

From this time on an odd visitor was coming to the Island. One Sunday at the beginning of July a canoe from

Dunquin brought a gentleman to the Blasket. He was a tall, lean, fair-complexioned, blue-eyed man. He had only a flavouring of Irish on his tongue. He went among the people and observed them, and in the evening he asked some of them whether he could find a place to stay. They told him he could, and he arranged to lodge in the King's house, and went back again without saying or doing anything else.

Not much of the Monday had gone when he had all his traps collected. He was asked what was the reason he didn't stay in Ballyferriter parish, and he said that there was too much English mixed with their Irish, and that didn't suit him; that his business was to get the fine flower of the speech, and that he had observed that the best Irish was here. He asked the King who was the best man to teach him Irish. The King explained to him that I was the man, for I was able to read it and had fine, correct Irish before ever I read it. He came to me at once and questioned me. He put a book before me, '*Niamh.*' 'You're all right, but have you got English?' says he.

'I haven't a great deal of English, sir,' says I to him.

'That'll do,' says he.

The first day we came together he gave me the style of 'master'.

This was Carl Marstrander. He was a fine man, with the same manner to low and high, and, methinks, that's always the way with so many of his sort who have great learning. He spent five months in the Blasket. One sitting a day we had for half that time, two or three hours every day; but he had news that he wouldn't have the time he'd thought at first, and then we had to change our plan. He put another question to me: Was it possible for me to spend two sittings a day with him?

It was after the day's work was done that I used to go to him, for the nights were long at that time of year. We were

WESTERN END OF THE ISLAND, INISH NA BRÓ AND
INISHVICKILLAUN IN THE DISTANCE

ABOVE THE GRAVEL STRAND, LOOKING TOWARDS
SYBIL HEAD

fishing and I had a boat with another man, and that wouldn't permit me to spend any time in his company that would interfere with the fishing. I could only have the second sitting with him in the day-time; but, all the same, how could I give the gentleman a refusal? I told him I'd do my best for him. So we went at it together, and, whenever I came in for my dinner I would go to him, and that wouldn't set me back in my fishing for long. It was just Christmas Eve when he got home after leaving us. He sent yellow gold to me when he had got home. I haven't heard anything from him for many a long day.

It was about the year 1909 when the Norseman Marstrander was with us. It was not long after that when Tadhg O'Ceallaigh came to us. He was a good Irish speaker. He used to have an Irish class in the schoolhouse for about two hours every night. I never let a night go by that I didn't spend with him.

It was at this very time that a letter came to me from the Norseman, full of paper, so that I could send to him in Norway the name of every animal on the land, of every bird in the sky, of every fish in the sea, and of every herb that grows; with orders that I was not to have recourse to any book, but to spell them after my own fashion.

Well, I hadn't too much practice in writing the language at this time, and I tell you, my lad, I'd have needed to be first-rate at it to spell all the names aright. I mentioned the matter to Tadhg O'Ceallaigh.

'O!' says he, 'we'll help one another, and do it splendidly.'

He wasn't slow to get to work, for the task delighted him beyond anything. We used to spend part of the day at them till we'd finished them and dispatched them overseas.

Tadhg only stayed a month.

The year after he left us fish was to be had plentifully every night they could go after them. A half-dozen boats from Dunquin used to come, too. They were as skilled at sea then as they have been ever since.

Well, it was a soft, calm, moist night, and every canoe we had put out to sea. The night went well till it was half spent. At midnight we made the creek and landed the boats high and dry. Every one of us went to his own house, and we had a bite of food. Then off we started again, and some of the boats went with us, while others whose crews had gone to bed never went out again at all, and some of the Dunquin boats didn't go back home, but remained at sea off the Blasket landing-place. The rain showed no sign of stopping. Off went every boat of us to work, some of them pretty far from home. As for our boat, it wasn't far from the land. We let go the nets, all we had in the canoe. They were only just spread out on the sea when we heard a noise coming our way, and what should it be but a squall. The blast was so fierce that it flung every one of us down off the thwart into the bottom of the canoe, and gave the canoe itself a good shaking.

I sprang to the rope that held the nets at the stern of the boat and fell to dragging on it till the nets were coming towards me. Then the wind went again as fast as it had come, and things eased off a bit. The other pair told me to look if there was any fish in the nets, and there was one here and there.

'Out with them back again,' said they, for not another breath of wind had come all this time.

The rope was but just taut again when there came another noise, seven times as loud as the last one, and it left no drop of water in the sea that it didn't lift into the air. It shook the canoe and tossed her this way and that.

'Be quick and jump and haul back the rope,' cried the pair. 'There will be a storm immediately.'

'We should have had it on board now right enough if

we'd only kept on that time,' says I. And I sprang to the rope at once.

It wasn't in my strength to haul in the breadth of my nail or an inch of the net. I had to face towards the stern of the canoe and set my heels against the foot-boards, and even so it came slow and stiff.

We got the net on board safe and sound; but there never was weather like it by this time, what with rain and wind. We were right to windward of the creek, making for home. One of us was rowing and the two others steering, and, though I had two iron thole pins in the stern, they were bent with the strain on them.

We were dragged to safety, for we had almost been carried past the harbour, struggle as we might. When we reached the harbour it was high tide, and it was a spring tide, and the place was crammed with boats as we came in, and the creek was very narrow.

When we put our rope ashore, we heard that a canoe had been driven east through the channel with only one man in her, a Dunquin man; that the other two of the crew had left him and got to land by leaping on to the rock when they came in without bringing a rope or anything ashore with them out of the canoe. The little canoe with the lone man in her drove east through the channel, and off it went through the stormy night. It was a terrible thing. Could anything be done? But nothing could.

The gale continued blowing out of all measure through the night, and the little canoe and the man were being swept before the wind through Dingle Bay until milking-time next day. Just at that point of the day he was blown into Valencia harbour, himself and his canoe, unhurt and undamaged. He was taken good care of there; he had passed all alone through the storm, and they marvelled that he had not died for very terror in the long, endless night.

When I had come home I must go out of doors again to

find out if my relations were safe at home; it was the children that put me to that trouble, for their uncles were on the sea, and how should they know whether they had been caught in the storm or not? A heavy rain was still falling unceasingly, and I had to crawl on hands and knees from one house to the other. At the very moment when I reached my own house the dawn was beginning and the rain stopping. I threw off my clothes and went to my bed, tired and weary, and soon I was dead asleep in it.

Two days after people went out from the Blasket to the land to keen the drowned man, for there was a sort of wake there. In the middle of the business who should come in at the door to them but the man himself. A steamship had brought him across to Dingle—himself, his canoe, and his nets. The story of this happening spread through the country, and before long somebody from the Government came and looked at the passage. When he had gone back, it wasn't long till they were at work, and the work went on till the passage was closed and raised higher than the land all round. This was going on for a good while. I got fifteen pounds for the work, and I only had one man's pay, and many a day I was not employed at all.

I was out fishing one night after the passage through the harbour had been set right. It was a fine night, and we had no need to go far from home. Anyhow we weren't getting much fish, and we rowed to the White Strand and made a cast of the nets. We hadn't had the nets out long when we noticed something floundering far back in the net. I said to the two others that there was a seal there, and if there were any mackerel there, he wouldn't be long about eating them; but the pair didn't pay much heed to what I had to say, letting it go in at one ear and out at the other. Soon after that the man in the bows said that there was some devil or other in the net, for he was dragging the net and the boat after him at full speed.

The word was hardly said when the thing in the net went mad. It dragged the nets and the boat for about a mile, and came near to drowning us at that effort, only there were twenty fathoms of rope tied to the end of the net, and I had to pay all that out down to the last bit that I held in my hand.

All we could do then was to let him have the nets, and that would be a great loss to a poor fisherman. The man in the bows told me to haul on the rope again. I did so, and we pulled a bit of the seine on board, and it was then that we began to talk to one another! It was a bright moonlight night, and when we saw the huge creature a bit back from the stern of the boat, the three of us went yellow with terror, utterly at a loss to know what we ought to do. The man in the bows told me not to let the nets go. He'd rather be drowned even than lose his nets.

We spent some time like this, and we had to let the net go back and forth. The great beast had the six nets all twisted round him except one net; and when he went down, we had to let the rope run every time till he struck the sand at the bottom. We were fighting him till we came near the landing-place. I had a good knife open all the time ready to draw it across the rope, but there would have been little help in that if the beast had run wild.

At last we reached the harbour, where we got help from two other canoes. The beast was as big as the whole harbour basin. Soon he wallowed all over the basin and drenched all of us that were there, and clouted the rock with his back fin. He split the rock and knocked half a ton out of it. He came near to frightening to death all in the harbour when he was landed. The liver in him provided the whole island with light for five years. It was a tough job to get the nets off him. He left us only the ropes of the nets, all the rest was torn and rent. The three of us have never been the same since; we'd had too great a fright; we should have been drowned if we hadn't been so close to the harbour.

Another day we had the canoe anchored to a stone and were fishing with the line. Soon a shark passed under the boat, swimming backwards and forwards without leaving it, and he couldn't be driven away. One of us was lying along the thwart, and, of course, his legs were stretching over the gunwale. I was in the stern of the boat, and, glancing down, what should I see but the shark with his jaws wide open, making, belly upwards, towards the feet. I shouted to the man in the boat's waist to draw in his legs. He did double quick. The shark reared up half out of the water, and he nearly sank us with the rush of it. We had to pull up anchor and make the land, and he followed us so long as he had two fathoms of water. We were no good for the rest of that day, and didn't get our courage back again for a week.

I've never seen a sea beast since floating on the surface of the water but my heart shook. It's often that a canoe or a boat has been sunk in the night-time, and often in the day, too, and the people could not make out what had befallen them. It is my belief that it is a monster of this kind that attacks them and overturns them. There's many a danger lying in wait for those that follow the sea.

24. *This and That*

ONE morning people were out early in this island, and what should there be to look at but a great, white tent on the cliff above the harbour in Dunquin. It seemed curious to us, although the landlord had been often threatening us before this. Some of us said that it was the bailiffs, others said no. Whatever the white house there on the land meant, none of us had much fancy for going out. Some of us were near to starving for lack of provisions.

There came a very fine day, and a middle-aged man who had a canoe of his own that wasn't an outsize said that he would go out if two lads would go with him. I told him he'd do better to stop at home, and that it was no good thing that was on the mainland. It was no use being at him since he'd got the idea into his head. He found the lads and started off across the Sound. He was a vainglorious, little fellow, with a bush, like a buck goat's, under his chin.

He never stopped or cooled till he struck Dunquin harbour. My man hurried up to view the tent, and found out at once that it was an army of invasion against the Blasket. He wasn't satisfied without seeing what sort of men it was who were in the white house. He went to where he could see the door opening, and caught sight of a gun or two. There was a man like himself in the tent, with a goat's beard like his own, and he saw that the man outside was a cheeky fellow from the way he was peering at him through the door, noticing everything. All he did was to snatch up his gun and point it at him.

When the man outside saw what he was at, he bolted from the white house and faced for the harbour, where he had his little canoe. The grey man with the gun followed him for a bit of fun, and he fired a shot to put the fear of death in his heart.

The islandman called the two lads to the canoe. They dragged it down after them from high-tide mark down to low-tide mark. They hadn't been long afloat when the lads noticed the sea-water welling up round their knees, and they screamed out that they were drowned!

Though they weren't far from the land, the old man wouldn't let them turn back for fear of the grey man with the gun. He shoved his vest into the hole the water was coming through, and set a boy to bail her until they reached their own harbour.

I happened to be waiting for them there. I asked the old man to give some account of what was on the land, but it was a surly answer I got: 'There they are for you. Go and see for yourself.'

'I told you not to go,' said I to him, 'for you're no good at home or abroad.' I lifted my fist and fetched him a clout in the ear-hole.

I'd given good advice to the rascal when he was setting out in the morning, and now it was the worst word in his mouth that he had for me when he got back. This wasn't the first time either that such a thing happened, and you see it made me so angry that I lifted my fist to him, the only time in the world that I ever did it to anybody. But the grey man with the gun put such a fright into him that he was never the same man again. When his tale about the bailiffs came to the ears of the Islanders, it worried us a lot. The most that lived there in those days were bitter poor. We were in a trap then, for we couldn't go ashore at all.

When the parish priest heard of it, he didn't like it, and he didn't rest till he could find out if there was any way of setting us free. The Congested Districts Board had been taking up estates in the countryside for some time before this. The priest made inquiries to see whether he could bring the Blasket under the Board. He was told that they were willing to take it on, and he sent a message to us to come out to him at once, for an officer of the Board would be with him on the day he had fixed. The day appointed was too stormy and we couldn't go to our usual harbour, but had to put in to Cuas an Reha. The pair were waiting for us with their backs against a rock.

We talked with them for a bit, and they with us, till they made it clear to us that we should never see the white house again, and, after we'd gone through a lot of explanations, we said farewell to one another. It wasn't a very good day on the sea for us, and though they were on dry land, it didn't deserve a word of praise from them either, for snow showers out of the north-west were blinding both of them and their horses. When we got to the Island, the whole population was down by the water waiting to see what news we had for them. We had good news, and gave it them with joy.

The next day the white house was down, and before long one man after another came to visit us from the Board. 'Tis an old saying that 'God's help is nearer than the door', also that 'the thing a man likes least in the world may be, for all he knows, the very heart of his fortune'. So it was with us in this matter of the white house. However hard our masters may be after us sometimes, the Great Master of all often sends them to the rightabout.

Before long the officer of the Board came. He put up a tent and spent some time among us measuring and apportioning the land. It was I who held the other end of the chain for him. He wrote down our names as tenants under the Board, and we were to be content with this and that. He brought a foreman with him and a lot of materials in a trawler from Dingle, and put a great deal of work in train. When he'd got everything arranged for the ganger, he left him in charge of the whole affair, meaning to pay visits to us himself now and again. A man used to come to pay wages once a fortnight.

The Board spent a year and a half working in the Blasket, and most of the men in the village were at work every week and every day. Two shillings a day was our pay—pretty good when we were working for ourselves.

Seventeen shillings a year was the rent on my holding, and still is, while my grandfather in the old days used to pay ten pounds. That's a great change in the world.

Five new houses were built in the Island. I and the ganger put up every inch of them, and often the two of us had to work desperately hard. We used a contraption of wooden boards for them, for they are built of mixed gravel and cement, and we had to keep them as straight as a gun barrel. Before they were finished that ganger was called away and he had to go, and another man came who hadn't the least notion of building houses. I had to finish them.

Among other misfortunes, this new ganger didn't understand a word of Irish. A day came when a floor was to be laid in one of the new houses, and there were four men working on a wooden platform mixing the mortar. The ganger wanted to give them an order to mix so much cement with so much gravel. The men mixing the mortar had no English and the ganger no Irish, and that made a mess of the work, and they fell out with one another. I was up under the slates plastering. Before long I saw him coming towards me in a bad temper.

'Come down here,' says he. 'These four at the board are as stupid as four asses.'

I came down a great, long ladder and went to the

platform, and found out the cause of the muddle. I told them what the ganger wanted done. The ganger was cursing away.

'Those are the four stupidest men I ever saw,' says he, 'and I'll have to discharge them.'

'But this is what the four say,' said I, 'that if the Board wants these houses finished, you'll have to be discharged and somebody put in your place who can make himself understood. A man like you can be no use here.'

The ganger never had so much to say after that as before. I fancy he realized that it was with him the fault lay.

The Board improved our holdings so that every man knows his own plot and has it fenced so that he can do his sowing in a part of it whenever he likes. It wasn't so with us before: unless your next neighbour was ready to sow with you, you had to stop, for you couldn't fence your plot; every man's allotment for sowing was too small.

We've never had any distraint for rent since that time, but I'm afraid it won't be so for ever. We are getting poorer every day.

When the land was all tidily settled by the Board and every man had his own field here and there, trimly fenced, there was nothing to prevent us sowing all we wanted, and we used to do that, and more. Before the Board came we hadn't proper fencing for these little fields, and in the little bits of land we did sow—often enough with good potatoes —we used to have pigs and asses, and they'd often make an utter mess of them after all our labour. Many a year I've spent in which I had to do a man's part in the day-time after being up all night, about All Souls' Day, after mackerel; and often enough I've spent a whole week without sleep till I had my potatoes in store. Now, when we had our gardens all ship-shape, so that neither deer nor eagle could go into them, nothing could tire us of sowing and reaping.

At this time there rose up a babbler amongst us, and his idea was to have food without sweat. He stuck his hands under his oxters. As happens with every villainy, it wasn't long till first one and then a pair of lads did as he did, and many of them started to take their ease. This ill-conditioned rascal told them that it was the same food one would get after all, and that only horses and fools worked in this world.

First one field, then two, and then three, went to ruin, and remained fallow without a thing planted in them. The man that started this rascality went to America, and he didn't find bread growing on the hedges there. We've never been so keen on planting since as we were at first, and the walls that the Board set up to fence the fields are beginning to fall.

One day I was fetching a load of turf on the hill, and what should I see but a trawler from Dingle sailing east on the south side of the Island. She had every sail in her set, and a strong gale was blowing out of the north. A fierce gust swept down the hill-side and I heard the clatter coming my way, but I gave no heed to it.

When it struck the ass that was just in front of me, it stripped the baskets off him and knocked him flat, and me, too, and drove all the wits out of my head. I sprang up and looked round me, but I couldn't find the baskets, though I found the ass. I looked after the baskets and saw the trawler, and was amazed when I saw no sails on her—only rags and tatters. The gust had swept them clean away. She lay there like a fool, never moving.

I looked closely and saw my baskets floating out in the great sea about twenty yards from the trawler that was stripped of her sails.

I stood a few minutes to think what I had best do. There wasn't a sod of turf in the house or anything to cook a thing, and my creels were gone! The plan I hit on was to take the two bags out of the ass's packstraddle and put the turf in them, one of them on either side of him.

In the matter of religious service, so far as my memory goes back, we had endless trouble. We must go across the Sound to Mass, three long miles to Dunquin. In winter the Sound is rarely fit for it, and we were forced, and still are, to stay at home. We were often a whole quarter without a Mass. Any Sunday we couldn't go out we used to say the rosary at the time when the Mass was being celebrated on the land.

As regards Confession, it's only a man here and there that would go out to Dunquin for it, so long as I can recall, but the priests came into the Island once a year. A big boat from Dunquin was appointed by the parish priest to bring them in, and he used to give them all the money that was collected for himself at the Station. That's how it used to be till these big boats went out of use and there were none of them remaining in the Island or out. Canoes from the Island bring them in ever since then.

Not half the respect is paid to the priests now that was paid in the days of my youth. When I was a boy, I remember well nobody was considered to have welcomed the priest properly who didn't put one knee to the ground after sweeping his cap right off his head. In the world of to-day if there is a gathering to meet the priest, those in front will doff their caps, but maybe not another cap will be doffed from there to the back. No woman was allowed to go in a boat with a priest in it, whatever her haste or need, and never one of them came near the landing-place. But, for some time now, there's none to say them nay if the boat is crammed with them.

One of the oldest recollections I have is seeing the bishop in the Blasket. I fancy the reason I took such note of him beyond anyone else was that he had a special mantle on, for I can't have been many years old. If anyone wants to know exactly where the episcopal seat is on the Blasket, it wouldn't take me long to put my finger on it. He went walking on after leaving the landing-place till he came to a green-grassed place. There was a rock in the middle of this place. The bishop stopped and looked about him and sat down on the rock, gathering his cloak about him. 'This place is just right, since the day is fine,' says he.

I don't remember any bishop coming since then. Once every three years for some time past the young folk are summoned to go out to the place where the parish priest lives in Ballyferriter to be confirmed by the bishop. A house used to be prepared in the Island for the Stations every year when they came; but so long as the school has been here they are held in it.

Many people have been coming to the Island for years in quest of Irish. Most of them spent a month here. I had to spend a time in the company of each one of them, and do my own work into the bargain. A man came to this Island, and he's come a good deal since. 'Bláithín' is what we call him. He is Robin Flower from London. He had heard from Carl Marstrander before he came that he had been with me. When this good fellow got to Ireland, he never rested till he reached the Great Blasket. He's been coming every year since. We used to spend the time together writing. We had two sittings every day at it. He spent some time every year in my company to get every word we had written arranged in order till it was right and easy. That book will tell of every disaster that befell round the Blaskets, both the little and the big: the strait that trapped some of the men, how some of them dwelt for a time in the little islands, how they fared in them, the wrecked ship, the fairy cry, and other apparitions that were to be seen often and often, if report speaks true of them.

The daughter I had—the one that survived that day on

the White Strand—had a relation in Dunmore, and this woman wanted her living near her. She married in Dunmore and had a good place there. Her going made a great gap for me. I had nobody then to look after things for me, but we were left to blunder on, dragging the world after us. I was but a dark, dispirited dullard after my daughter left me. A dozen years she lived in Dunmore after that. She left six young children behind her. Whatever sorrow else befell me, that sorrow of the grave was the crown of them all.

The Great War hadn't been going on for long when ships were being wrecked and destroyed on the ocean and strangers were coming in open boats from every quarter of the sea. The only person I had in the house with me at that time was my brother Pats, who was twelve years older than I was. He had his pension then.

There's no telling of all the goods that were adrift on the surface of the sea while the war was going on. Two miles from the harbour here a great ship ran upon the rocks. The *Quebra* she was called. Her captain said that she had in her cargo everything that feeds mankind except drink. And he was right. The sea filled up with everything eye had ever seen and that we had never seen in this place. Hundreds of pounds' worth was salvaged from the wreck, and the Islanders made a great deal of money out of her, though they didn't get what they ought.

I had nothing to do but to watch them, to be sure, for I went neither in boat nor in bark, and nobody invited me.

While the Great War was on Brian O'Ceallaigh came to me. He spent a year with us, and he was in our company for Christmas that year. When he had gone, I used to send him a journal every day for five years. Then nothing would satisfy him but that I should write of my own life and tell him how I had passed my days.

It was never my way to refuse anybody, so I set about

the job. What you're reading now, reader, is the fruit of my labours. I was putting the world past me like this for some time more; people coming in ones and twos and threes, and every one of them having his own sittings with me.

The Gaelic League had been founded five years when I put my head into it, and, however hard I'd worked, I've been working harder year by year, and to-day I go harder at it than ever for the sake of the language of our country and of our ancestors.

Father Clune came and spent three weeks with me. He said Mass for us every day. He came back again, and I was a month in his company. We helped one another, correcting all the words in 'Réilthíní Óir'. We used to be sitting at it eight hours a day in two sessions—four hours in the morning and four in the afternoon—for all that month. That's the most painful month's work I ever did, on land or sea.

One of my sons had been in America for twelve years. He came home about this time, himself and his wife and two children. He was on the same ship as Archbishop Mannix when he was taken out of the ship. He only stayed with me half a year when he started across the water again and left me. There was no fishing or anything when they came, but they spent the pound or two that they had brought with them, and what he said was that, if things went on as they were going much longer, he'd have spent every penny he brought with him, or that might be coming to him, and that he'd have nothing left at home or abroad. And I think he was right! My brother, the old pensioner, left me when they came home. He was received into a house in Dunquin, and is still there, in his eightieth year.

I have another young son with me, and he has to stay around the house, for there is little good in me except in my tongue. We have neither cow nor horse, sheep nor lamb, canoe nor boat. We have a handful of potatoes and a fire. I have been twenty-seven years hard at work on this language, and it is seventeen years since the Norseman, Marstrander, came my way. Something or other comes to me now and again, one thing after another, that keeps me from starvation. I hear many an idle fellow saying that there's no use in our native tongue; but that hasn't been my experience. Only for it I should have been begging my bread!

25. *The End*

WELL, I've slipped along thus far to the end of my story. I have set down nothing but the truth; I had no need of invention, for I had plenty of time, and have still a good deal in my head. It's amazing what a lot there is in an old man's head when somebody else starts him talking and puts questions to him. All the same, what I've written down are the things that meant most to me. I considered the whole course of my life, and the things that had meant most to me were the first to come back to memory.

I have brought other people besides myself into my story, for, if I hadn't, it would have been neither interesting nor complete. I never disliked any of them, and I've spent my life in their company till to-day without any trouble between us. I don't know what colour the inside walls of the court in Dingle are, old though I am.

We are poor, simple people, living from hand to mouth. I fancy we should have been no better off if we had been misers. We were apt and willing to live, without repining, the life the Blessed Master made for us, often and again ploughing the sea with only our hope in God to bring us through. We had characters of our own, each different from the other, and all different from the landsmen; and we had our own little failings, too. I have made no secret of our good traits or of our little failings either, but I haven't told all the hardships and the agonies that befell us from time to time when our only resource was to go right on.

This is a crag in the midst of the great sea, and again and again the blown surf drives right over it before the violence of the wind, so that you daren't put your head out any more than a rabbit that crouches in his burrow in

Inishvickillaun when the rain and the salt spume are flying. Often would we put to sea at the dawn of day when the weather was decent enough, and by the day's end our people on land would be keening us, so much had the weather changed for the worse. It was our business to be out in the night, and the misery of that sort of fishing is beyond telling. I count it the worst of all trades. Often and again the sea would drive over us so that we could see the land no more—a long, long night of cold like this, struggling against the sea, with often little to get, only praying from moment to moment for the help of God. It was rare, indeed, for us to get a full catch, and then often we would have to cut away the nets and let it all go with the sea. On other nights, after all the labour of the fishing, the boats would be fairly full, and we couldn't make the harbour or the land, but the swell would be rising to the green grass, the storm blowing out of the north-west, and the great waves breaking. We would have to flee then before the gale, some of us to Cuan Croumha, some to Ventry harbour, some to Dingle.

You may understand from this that we are not to be put in comparison with the people of the great cities or of the soft and level lands. If we deserved blame a little at times, it would be when a drop of drink was going round among us. The drink went to our heads the easier because we were always worn and weary, as I have described, like a tired horse, with never any rest or intermission.

It was a good life in those days. Shilling came on shilling's heels; food was plentiful, and things were cheap. Drink was cheap, too. It wasn't thirst for the drink that made us want to go where it was, but only the need to have a merry night instead of the misery that we knew only too well before. What the drop of drink did to us was to lift up the hearts in us, and we would spend a day and a night ever and again in company together when we got the chance. That's all gone by now, and the high heart and the fun are passing from the world. Then we'd take the homeward way together easy and friendly after all our revelry, like the children of one mother, none doing hurt or harm to his fellow.

I have written minutely of much that we did, for it was my wish that somewhere there should be a memorial of it all, and I have done my best to set down the character of the people about me so that some record of us might live after us, for the like of us will never be again.

I am old now. Many a thing has happened to me in the running of my days until now. People have come into the world around me and have gone again. There are only five older than me alive in the Island. They have the pension. I have only two months to go till that date—a date I have no fancy for. In my eyes it is a warning that death is coming, though there are many people who would rather be old with the pension than young without it.

I can remember being at my mother's breast. She would carry me up on to the hill in a creel she had for bringing home the turf. When the creel was full of turf, she would come back with me under her arm. I remember being a boy; I remember being a young man; I remember the bloom of my vigour and my strength. I have known famine and plenty, fortune and ill-fortune, in my life-days till to-day. They are great teachers for one that marks them well.

One day there will be none left in the Blasket of all I have mentioned in this book—and none to remember them. I am thankful to God, who has given me the chance to preserve from forgetfulness those days that I have seen with my own eyes and have borne their burden, and that when I am gone men will know what life was like in my time and the neighbours that lived with me.

Since the first fire was kindled in this island none has

written of his life and his world. I am proud to set down my story and the story of my neighbours. This writing will tell how the Islanders lived in the old days. My mother used to go carrying turf when I was eighteen years of age. She did it that I might go to school, for rarely did we get a chance of schooling. I hope in God that she and my father will inherit the Blessed Kingdom; and that I and every reader of this book after me will meet them in the Island of Paradise.

THE GREAT BLASKET
1926